CREATIVE
HOMEOWNER®

the Earth Friendly DISCARD Home

Nancy Hajeski
Jennifer Acker
Philip J. Schmidt
David Goucher
and others

CREATIVE HOMEOWNER®, Upper Saddle River, New Jersey

COPYRIGHT © 2008 Hylas Publishing LLC
First published in North America by

HOMEOWNER®

A Division of Federal Marketing Corp.
Upper Saddle River, NJ

Trademark notices appear on page 237.

The Earth-Friendly Home was produced for Creative Homeowner by Hylas Publishing LLC, 129 Main Street, Irvington, NY 10533
www.hylaspublishing.com

THE EARTH-FRIENDLY HOME

SENIOR EDITOR Suzanne Lander
ART DIRECTOR Brian MacMullen
DESIGN AND LAYOUT Lisa Purcell
JUNIOR EDITOR Rachael Lanicci
EDITORIAL ASSISTANT Gabrielle Kappes
INDEXER Casey Tolfree
JUNIOR DESIGNERS Hwaim Holly Lee, Eunoh Lee
PHOTO COORDINATOR Ben DeWalt
FRONT COVER DESIGN Glee Barre

CREATIVE HOMEOWNER

VICE PRESIDENT AND PUBLISHER Timothy O. Bakke
ART DIRECTOR David Geer
MANAGING EDITOR Fran J. Donegan

Current Printing (last digit)
10 9 8 7 6 5 4 3 2 1

Manufactured in the United States of America

The Earth-Friendly Home, First Edition
Library of Congress Control Number: 2008922038
ISBN 10: 1-58011-429-6
ISBN 13: 978-1-58011-429-5

CREATIVE HOMEOWNER®
A Division of Federal Marketing Corp.
24 Park Way
Upper Saddle River, NJ 07458
www.creativehomeowner.com

Planet Friendly Publishing
✔ Made in the United States
✔ Printed on Recycled Paper
Learn more at www.greenedition.org

GREEN EDITION

At Creative Homeowner we're committed to producing books in an earth-friendly manner and to helping our customers make greener choices.

Manufacturing books in the United States ensures compliance with strict environmental laws and eliminates the need for international freight shipping, a major contributor to global air pollution.

And printing on recycled paper helps minimize our consumption of trees, water, and fossil fuels. *The Earth-Friendly Home* was printed on paper made with 10% post-consumer waste. According to Environmental Defense's Paper Calculator, by using this innovative paper instead of conventional papers, we achieved the following environmental benefits:

Trees Saved: 21

Water Saved: 7,610 gallons

Solid Waste Eliminated: 1,259 pounds

Air Emissions Eliminated: 2,322 pounds

For more information on our environmental practices, please visit us online at www.creativehomeowner.com/green

SOLAR ENERGY

EFFICIENT LIGHTING

RENEWABLE ENERGY

INSULATION

SAVING ENERGY

EARTH-FRIENDLY HOME

ENERGY STAR APPLIANCES

BACK TO BASICS

NATURAL RESOURCES

HIGH-MILEAGE CARS

Contents

THERE ARE PROBABLY SEVERAL REASONS behind your decision to make your home earth friendly. It may have started with a personal conviction that you want to live a more conscientious lifestyle. You may be a practical person who doesn't like to waste anything. Perhaps your home is due for an update, and you want to make improvements that won't have a negative impact on the planet. Maybe you want to replace old appliances with ones that will run cleaner and more efficiently. You might have health issues that require you to remove chemicals and other toxins from your home's interior. Saving money on heating and cooling costs could certainly be a consideration. Alternatively, you might want to start setting a better example for your children or grandchildren when it comes to using resources wisely. Whatever the reasons for making your home a greener place, you'll reap several added benefits—you will be saving energy, reducing waste, and significantly shrinking your carbon footprint.

Creating a truly green home should involve all aspects of your daily life—the food you eat, the furniture and materials you decorate with, the way you garden, the car you drive, and the things you shop for. Your family's green consciousness will soon spill over to their office spaces or college dorms.

In the following chapters you'll discover many ways to turn your home into an oasis of green—with sustainable building materials and eco-friendly products. You'll learn how to gauge your current energy use—your carbon footprint—and find ways to reduce it. You'll also learn about all the kinds of renewable energy, some of which can be used to generate electricity on a large scale, as well as power individual homes. Finally, you can keep track of all of your energy-saving efforts with our handy checklists. You'll be able to mark off the progress you've made and be reminded of the things you can still do.

Ultimately, when you show guests around your earth-friendly home, you can do it with pride—because you have made wise and healthy choices for your family, as well as provided an example to others.

Chapter 1

THE GREEN HOME

Making Your House Earth Friendly

LIKE CHARITY, GREEN AWARENESS begins at home. Even the simplest changes that you make to improve energy conservation can have positive effects on the environment. Something as basic as not letting the water run while you brush your teeth or turning your thermostat down a few degrees can make a difference. Green is popping up all over—look at that aisle of eco-friendly products at the home improvement store or those energy-efficient appliances prominently displayed at the local appliance outlet. If there are children in your house, ask them to become part of the effort. Schedule a weekly recycling day, and let them keep the money from bottle and can deposits. Have them pack up toys and clothing that they no longer use to donate to charity. Keep a checklist on the fridge, marking off all the ways they've contributed. Make sure that they understand how important it is not to waste the resources of the fragile planet that they are going to inherit.

What Is a Green Home?

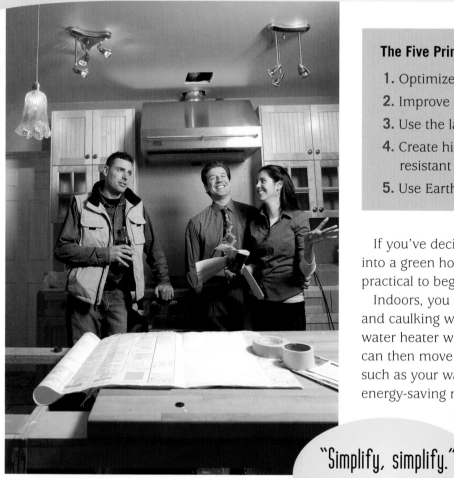

Planning and creating an energy-efficient house can be affordably financed through a number of federal- and state-run programs.

"Simplify, simplify."

—Henry David Thoreau

The Five Principles of Sustainable Design

1. Optimize use of the sun
2. Improve indoor air quality
3. Use the land responsibly
4. Create high-performance, moisture-resistant houses
5. Use Earth's natural resources wisely

If you've decided you want to turn your house into a green home, it might be easier and more practical to begin with one area at a time.

Indoors, you can start by improving insulation and caulking windows and pipe entries. Wrap your water heater with a special insulating blanket. You can then move on to replacing old appliances, such as your washer and dryer or dishwasher, with energy-saving models. Any time you are doing a spruce up on the walls or cabinets, make sure you use water-based or milk paints. You might get a decade or two more out of that hardwood floor by sanding and refinishing it. If you are replacing flooring or carpeting, opt for renewable woods, such as bamboo, and natural fibers, such as cotton or wool, that are not treated with chemicals. Also remember to properly dispose of everything that can't be recycled.

IDEALLY A GREEN HOME INCORPORATES sustainable or recycled building materials, uses renewable energy sources wherever possible, and relies on eco-friendly appliances, paints, cleaning products, and furnishings.

The residents of a green home have decided to alter their lifestyle in order to live more efficiently. They have taken stock of their habits and activities and found numerous ways to conserve energy, shrink waste, and sharply reduce their carbon footprint. They have also discovered that a green house is healthy for its occupants and relatively inexpensive to run. A green house is beneficial for the environment as well.

Outdoors in the garden, you can begin by switching to natural fertilizers and pesticides. How about starting a compost pile for your organic waste? You can also plant trees or shrubs on your northern exposure to act as a natural windbreak. If you allow a corner of your lawn to "go wild," it may provide a habitat for wildlife, birds, and butterflies. If you plant a vegetable garden, you can barter the extra produce with your neighbors.

Ten Reasons to Live in a Green House

1. A green home saves money because it is energy efficient.

2. The air inside a green home is healthier; there are few chemical emissions from cabinetry, carpeting, paints, and fabrics.

3. Green building materials are often safer and more long lasting than traditional building materials.

4. Green homes help preserve old-growth forests because they utilize renewable resources, such as bamboo, wheatgrass, and cork, as well as lumber recycled from old buildings.

5. The green home aids in water conservation with its porous driveway and walkways, which allow drainage, and its drought-resistant garden plants.

6. The exterior of a green home needs less maintenance and repair because it incorporates vinyl and composite siding and trim, recycled composite decking, and durable stone and slate walkways.

7. The properly caulked green home is virtually airtight and draft free.

8. The addition of the homeowner's own compost to the soil around the green home makes it more fertile, and the elimination of chemical fertilizers and insecticides makes it healthier.

9. The green home reduces fossil fuel emissions by using local materials whenever possible, which eliminates long-distance transport.

10. The green home reduces the amount of refuse going to landfills by using recycled or salvaged materials.

Source: www.dreamspacesonline.com

BUILDING WITH THE FUTURE IN MIND

Whether you are constructing a house from scratch or doing renovations to an existing house or apartment, there is now a wide range of green building materials and products available, ones that do not destroy old-growth forests or the freshwater supply. The key attributes to look for in green building materials are renewability, reusability, and durability. Try to stay away from any products that require excess energy to extract them, process them, or ship them. You especially want to avoid products that negatively impact the outdoor or indoor environment of your home.

Owners of solar houses hooked up to the energy grid can sell excess electricity back to the local provider.

The Glidehouse

THE GREEN HOUSE: NEW DIRECTIONS IN SUSTAINABLE ARCHITECTURE AND DESIGN at the National Building Museum in Washington, D.C., ran from May 2006 to June 2007.

This exhibit featured a full-scale replica of architect Michelle Kaufmann's Glidehouse. Visitors got a first-hand experience of what it might be like to live in a green house, one that incorporated solar heat plus eco-friendly furnishings and building materials.

This kitchen combines PaperStone countertops, sustainably grown wood cabinetry, and energy-efficient lighting and appliances.

Built in a factory, the Glidehouse embraces the most modern and eco-friendly building methods and materials available.

Sliding doors and windows maximize natural light and breezes, while built-in storage minimizes clutter.

A Glidehouse comes ready to run on solar. A photovoltaic system can be incorporated during delivery or installed later.

Sliding dual-paned doors opposite clerestory windows create ample cross-ventilation and abundant natural lighting.

On warm days, the sliding glass doors and windows above can be opened to allow for cross-ventilation.

Built with long-lasting environmentally friendly materials, the Glidehouse requires little maintenance.

Though the Glidehouse conforms to Energy Star program standards for energy-efficient homes, as well as the American Lung Association Health House program, it can be built at a price consistent with or less than traditional onsite construction.

The prefabricated modular Glidehouse, designed so that it can be erected anywhere, generates comparatively little construction waste and can be positioned onsite to maximize solar gain in the summer and minimize heat loss in the winter. The house's narrow footprint provides cross-ventilation in all of its rooms. The window placement allows maximum solar benefits, and the clerestory window reduces the need for artificial light. The house is also airtight, lowering the cost of heating and cooling. The floors throughout are bamboo, a fast-growing, easily renewable material. The kitchen countertops are a lightweight concrete made of recycled newspaper and fly ash. The cabinets are free of toxic formaldehyde, and all appliances are energy-smart, as is the tankless water heater.

The Benefits of Modular Building

- Shortened construction time frame
- Predictable time and cost for the modular portions
- Prepackaged green solutions
- Marketability of green solutions and high quality designs

Source: Michelle Kaufmann Design, 2008

INSULATE
A high-performance air-barrier, open-cell foam insulation, coupled with caulked wood-to-wood framing joints, yields air-tight energy efficiency and reduces the risk of mold.

COOL EFFICIENTLY
Ceiling fans effectively circulate the air to create a breeze throughout the room, sometimes enabling you to avoid using the AC altogether.

ECO-FRIENDLY FLOORING
Reclaimed lumber or natural flooring such as bamboo, cork, or natural linoleum, is nontoxic and easier to maintain than other options.

CROSS-VENTILATE
Windows on two, three, or more sides lessen the expense of both heating and cooling. They also reduce the need to turn on lights during the day.

TRY COMPACT FLUORESCENTS
Compact fluorescent lights (CFLs) use one-quarter to one-third as much electricity as incandescent bulbs and last up to 10 times longer.

MODERATE YOUR TEMPERATURES
Dual- and triple-paned sliding doors allow cool breezes in summer and good insulation during colder weather.

GET PAPERSTONE
Harder than wood and stain resistant, PaperStone is a composite made from recycled paper and proprietary, petroleum-free phenolic resins made from cashew nut shell liquid.

Some Common Objections to Going Green

THE WHOLE CONCEPT OF GREEN BUILDING sprang up in response to people's increasing desire to live in homes that were more in harmony with the environment—and at the same time didn't deplete it. These green pioneers weren't necessarily rabid tree huggers; they also understood that green building was economically sound and a healthier alternative to traditional construction methods. Yet the ecological motives were always there—build something that won't increase carbon emissions, that won't dissipate energy, and that won't increase waste. These green homeowners bought into the whole package.

Sometimes, though, it takes a while for an idea to sink in on a larger scale, and so as the owner of a green—or potentially green—home, you're bound to meet up with skeptics who don't believe there's any urgent need to change the way we live. It's not your responsibility to convert them; it's more effective to set a good example.

Maybe you were once a skeptic yourself. You might have rationalized that any real danger to the planet was a long way off. Or you convinced yourself that science would come up with a way

Is Solar Energy Too Expensive?

Consider the sun! The most economical of all lighting is sunlight, which offers some of the least expensive and most flattering illumination of all. Researchers are finally starting to recognize the important role that ultraviolet light plays in human health. As a result, natural light is becoming a very important component of homes and office buildings. Studies have shown that when people live and work in a well-lit environment, they are happier, healthier, and more productive. Benefits of natural light include improved moods, increased energy levels, reduced eyestrain, truer color rendering, and more-spacious-appearing home interiors.

to eliminate greenhouse gases just in the nick of time. Perhaps you really wanted to make your home more green, but feared it would be too time-consuming and too expensive.

Quite likely you used the excuse most people fall back on: *What difference can I make? I'm only one person!*

It's true that one person can't do it alone, but if every household in the United States replaced a *single* regular light bulb with a fluorescent bulb, the energy saved could be used to light more than 2.5 million homes *for an entire year,* as well as

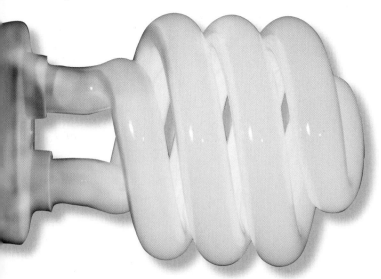

Each compact fluorescent reduces carbon dioxide emissions by more than 1,000 pounds over its lifetime.

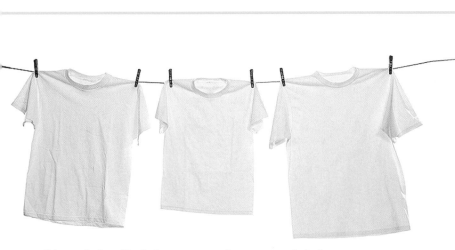

If instead of tumble-drying, you use solar energy and air dry your laundry on a line, your clothes will smell better and last longer.

reducing greenhouse gases roughly equivalent to the emissions of more than 750,000 cars.

What if you began washing your laundry in cold water and hanging it out in the sunshine to dry? A recent study by Cambridge University's Institute of Manufacturing reported that 60 percent of the energy associated with a piece of clothing is spent washing and drying it. A lone T-shirt can create up to 9 pounds of carbon dioxide during its lifetime. Cold washing and line drying can reduce the CO_2 output of your laundry by up to 90 percent. Imagine the result if every household in the United States gave that a try.

So there are things you can do—by taking a stand, acting on your convictions, and becoming an example to others. With a firm commitment to go green, you—and your home—will become part of the solution, rather than part of the problem.

> "You can either take action or you can hang back and hope for a miracle. Miracles are great, but they are so unpredictable."
>
> —Peter Drucker

The Many Shades of Green

There are various levels of commitment people are willing to make to support environmental issues. The green spectrum ranges from people who bike to work one day a week, homeowners who install solar heating panels, companies that offer eco-friendly products, to political activists who battle industrial polluters. At the far end of the spectrum are the eco-terrorists who bomb slaughterhouses and sawmills.

As a homeowner with a desire to raise your "green quotient," you may find that it's easier to start small rather than attempt a complete overhaul of your house. Typically, one positive action begets another, and you'll soon realize that your wasteful habits regarding energy, water, and other resources have changed for the better. Once incremental green thinking takes hold, you'll have a whole list of projects you'll want to undertake. The installation of sustainable wood cabinets in the kitchen, for instance, may lead to replacing the wall-to-wall carpeting in your living room with bamboo flooring. You may discover that recycling leads to composting, composting leads to growing your own vegetables, and the great taste of those vegetables leads you to start buying more varieties of organic or locally grown foods.

Chapter 2

TAKING STOCK
Your Home Energy Needs

FOOD, CLOTHING, SHELTER—the three basic human needs. Modern humans also require a source of heat in cool climates and a space to prepare meals, as well as places to sleep, bathe, and wash clothing—including all the fixtures and appliances that go with those activities. Many of us also want spaces for relaxing, entertaining, or pursuing hobbies. By the dawn of the twenty-first century, the emphasis has been less on basic necessities (needs) and more on what could be considered luxuries (wants). To begin paring down in preparation for creating a green, energy-efficient home, start by taking a personal inventory, separating your wants from your needs. Ask yourself: are there conveniences I can live without? Remind yourself that conspicuous consumption is the opposite of green thinking, which encourages people to reuse, recycle, renovate, restore, and refurbish the things that they already own.

Your Carbon Footprint

AMERICAN HOMES GENERATE **20** PERCENT of the United States' emissions. If you are a homeowner who's opted for a greener lifestyle, you're helping to reduce that number, which ultimately shrinks your own carbon footprint. But what exactly is a "carbon footprint," and how does it affect the planet?

Simply put, your carbon footprint is the impact you—or any individual—has on the environment in a given year based on the amount of greenhouse gas you produce as a result of burning fossil fuels. A carbon footprint is measured in units of carbon dioxide (CO_2), which is one of the most prevalent greenhouse gases. Greenhouse gases are emissions that rise into the earth's lower atmosphere and trap energy from the sun, preventing it from escaping the planet's atmosphere. In order of abundance, they are water vapor, carbon dioxide, methane, nitrous oxide, ozone, and CFCs (chlorofluorocarbon compounds, such as refrigerants, propellants, and cleaning solvents).

The heat trapped by these gases causes the phenomenon called global warming, a rise in the planet's temperature that can negatively impact climate. In the past, the forests have absorbed much of the carbon dioxide generated by the planet because plants "breathe" in carbon dioxide and emit oxygen. Now the human carbon footprint comprises half the total demand placed on earth's regenerative capacity. Though things like the production of alternative fuels, such as ethanol, show progress, there's still more to do.

WHAT'S YOUR SIZE?

If you want to calculate your own carbon footprint, several Web sites allow you to do this. (http://green.msn.com/ or Conservation.org/CarbonCalculator.) When assessing your carbon footprint, remember that you are responsible for not just the local, or direct onsite emissions, but also the ones called indirect emissions—categorized as offsite, external,

The Statistics of Waste

• Appliances, including heating and cooling equipment and water heaters, consume 90 percent of all energy used in the United States residential sector.

• An estimated 100 million barrels of oil were used in 2007 to make the plastic bags used in stores.

• If every household in the United States replaced one roll of 1,000-sheet bathroom tissues with 100-percent recyclable rolls, we could save 373,000 trees, 1.48 million cubic feet of landfill space, and 155 million gallons of water.

• The average meal in the United States travels more than 1,200 miles from the farm to your plate.

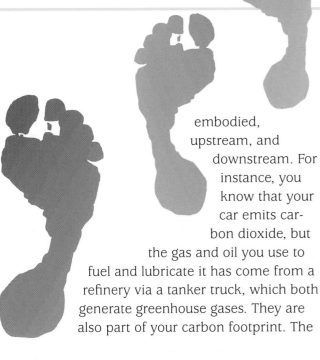

embodied, upstream, and downstream. For instance, you know that your car emits carbon dioxide, but the gas and oil you use to fuel and lubricate it has come from a refinery via a tanker truck, which both generate greenhouse gases. They are also part of your carbon footprint. The food you eat, the clothing you wear, the magazines and books you read—in fact, anything that has been transported long distances to reach you—are all part of that footprint.

Reducing Your Carbon Footprint

WHATEVER YOUR REASONS for deciding to create an earth-friendly home, once you begin to go green, you automatically start decreasing your carbon dioxide emissions. As with most attempts at improving the way you live, such as dieting or exercising, identifying the culprits is a lot easier than eliminating them. Just remember that change doesn't happen overnight. Some people start by refusing to add to their carbon footprint. You'll soon discover that there are numerous simple changes that you can make in your life to significantly shrink it.

Here are some tips and suggestions for living more sustainably and reducing the amount of energy you use.

AROUND THE HOUSE

- Insulate, weatherize, and air seal your home, and install energy-efficient heating and cooling systems. These steps can save up to 50 percent of your home heating and cooling bills.

- Switch ceiling fans to the reverse setting in winter to disperse rising heat.

- Install programmable thermostats that automatically adjust the temperature at night and when you are away from home.

- Turn down your thermostat by two degrees in winter and up one degree in summer—68°F in winter and 72°F in summer are optimum.

- Don't run window air-conditioning units unless the interior temperature reaches 80°F. Use ceiling, window, or box fans instead.

- Insulating your water heater allows it to work better and saves you energy costs.

- Turn down the thermostat on your hot water heater to 120°F.

Your Energy-Use Diary

One good way to get an idea of how much energy you really use is to keep a journal. During one week, write down everything you do that involves the use of some form of energy. Don't forget that every item you buy and every trip you make are part of that equation. Pay special attention to "stealth" energy drains—such as your cell phone charger that gets left on, even after you've removed the phone from the dock. Once you've pinpointed the many ways you're adding to your carbon footprint, you can begin addressing them.

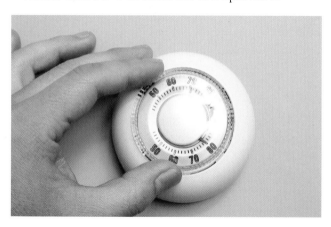

- Obtain electricity from a renewable energy source either by generating it directly—installing solar panels on your roof, for example—or by selecting an approved green energy provider.

IN THE KITCHEN

- Conserve energy by purchasing major appliances that have an EnergyStar rating.
- Scrape plates instead of rinsing them before loading the dishwasher. With today's new dishwashers and detergents, rinsing should not be necessary, plus it can use up more water than the entire wash cycle.
- Use your dishwasher only when it's full.
- Use larger appliances after 8 PM to reduce energy strain during peak hours.

- Instead of drinking bottled water—with the specter of all those plastic bottles lingering forever in a landfill—install water filters on your faucets or use a countertop filter system.
- Check your refrigerator door seal by placing a lit flashlight inside. Turn off the room light, and see if any light is escaping through the door. A damaged seal should be adjusted or replaced.
- Clean your refrigerator condenser coils at least once a year.
- Keep the refrigerator door open as briefly as possible. Keep your refrigerator temperature at 36° to 38°F and your freezer at 0° to 3°F.

- Use cloth napkins instead of paper ones. If a family of five each used a paper napkin at every meal, they would go through more than 5,400 in one year.
- Turn on the oven only 10 minutes before you need it.
- Add timers and automated thermostats to control appliance usage.
- Select solid woods for furniture or cabinetry, rather than pressed woods or composites that may contain formaldehyde or other toxic chemicals.

IN THE BATH

- Repair leaky fixtures and install low-flow shower-heads and faucets.
- Do not let the water run when brushing your teeth, shaving, or washing your face.
- Buy toilet paper and paper products made from recycled material; they help protect forests and reduce air and water pollution.

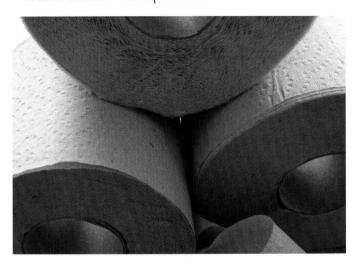

- Take showers instead of baths, unless your showers run more than 10 minutes.
- Install a tankless toilet.
- Use white vinegar as an all-around household cleaner in the kitchen and bathroom. It's safe to use around children and pets, and the sharp smell disappears in seconds.

IN LIVING AREAS

- Switch to compact fluorescent light bulbs, which significantly reduce electric consumption.
- Unplug all electronics that have an "instant start" feature, such as your TV or DVD player.
- Use wall coverings that are made of paper or natural fiber and are printed with natural inks.
- Opt for carpeting, rugs, window treatments, and other textiles made from untreated natural fibers, such as cotton or wool, which are free of toxins, pesticides, and chemical cleaners.
- Choose flooring products made from rapidly renewable resources, such as bamboo, cork, and natural linoleum.
- Increase natural lighting with additional windows, transoms, and skylights.

- Consider flooring or paneling with reclaimed wood products salvaged from older structures or certified wood harvested from sustainably managed forests.

IN THE WORKSHOP

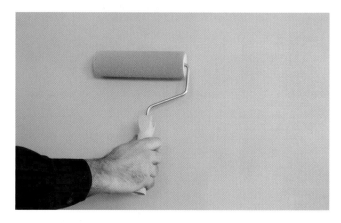

- Use water-based paints, finishes, and sealants or milk-based paints.
- Safely dispose of paint cans and other partially full containers whose contents could contaminate ground water.
- Use recycled rags for cleanups instead of paper towels, which add to the landfill.

LANDSCAPING AND EXTERIORS

- Reuse materials, such as brick, stone, glass, tile, and metal.
- Replace outdoor lighting with motion detectors that automatically turn off after a few minutes.
- Install awnings over exterior windows exposed to direct sunlight to lower cooling costs.
- Plant trees on your property. Trees can store between 5 and 400 pounds of carbon dioxide annually, depending on their size and growth rate. Properly placed trees also shade homes and low-rise apartment buildings, reducing air conditioning needs by up to 20 percent.

> "A small group of thoughtful people could change the world. Indeed, it's the only thing that ever has."
>
> —Margaret Mead

IN THE LAUNDRY

- Hang laundry on an outdoor clothesline or an indoor drying rack, instead of using an electric dryer.
- Use the cold or warm cycle of your washing machine whenever practical, and monitor dryer cycles.
- Use the moisture sensor on the dryer and clean the lint filter before each load.
- Dry heavier fabrics separately from lighter-weight fabrics.

FOOD PREP TIPS

- Make extra servings of dishes that refrigerate, freeze, and reheat well, such as stews, soups, and casseroles.
- Serve portions appropriate to your family's appetite to avoid waste.
- Use a microwave oven when possible; it uses less energy than a conventional oven and cooks 75 percent faster.

- Freeze leftover bread, rolls, or muffins, rather than storing them in the refrigerator, to keep them from going stale.

- Don't boil an entire kettle of water to make one cup of tea or coffee.
- Put a lid on cooking pots to reduce energy usage by 20 percent.
- Wash fruits and vegetables in a bowl of water instead of under running water.
- Put vegetable scraps and chicken or meat trimmings and bones into a freezer bag for making soup stock.
- Add old vegetables and all trimmings into a compost pile.
- Pack your children's lunch in an insulated bag rather than wasting a brown bag every day.

BUYING TIPS

- Purchase only enough produce to last a week, and put the most perishable items on the menu first.

- Consider the "life cycle" of furnishings and accessories before purchasing. Choose ones made of materials that can be reused or recycled when the item eventually wears out.

- Recycle all packing and shipping materials from any newly purchased items.

   - Don't buy fruit or vegetables wrapped in polystyrene foam and plastic—and skip the plastic produce bags.

      - Follow the European tradition of bringing your own carry bags with you when you shop for groceries.

- Buy locally produced products and materials to reduce the energy use and pollution associated with transporting them.

- Eliminate waste by choosing products that are biodegradable or recyclable.

GENERAL LIFESTYLE TIPS

- Recycle paper, plastic, glass, and aluminum cans. When possible, purchase recycled products.

- Carry a reusable coffee cup to work or while on the go. One plastic mug used twice a day instead of two disposable cups can save 135 pounds of carbon dioxide emissions per person per year.

- Use a real cup at home or work.

- Monitor your garbage output; a 10 percent reduction decreases carbon dioxide emissions by 1,200 pounds.

- Consider going meatless one day a week. Meat production requires much more energy than growing vegetables and grains, and the livestock industry is responsible for 18 percent of greenhouse gases. If every American went meat-free one day a week, it would reduce emissions equivalent to taking 8 million cars off the roads.

- Hand down outgrown clothing to relatives or friends, or donate them to a thrift store or a charitable organization.

Reducing a carbon footprint, whether for an individual or for a corporation, requires these three basic steps:

1. Identify all the areas where you might be contributing to carbon dioxide emissions.
2. Eliminate as many of those areas as possible.
3. Find ways to neutralize the carbon dioxide emissions that cannot be eliminated.

- Make sure you dispose of batteries and electronic devices in the recommended manner. Carelessly discarded computers can leech lead and other contaminants into the soil.
- Opt for train travel, when possible, instead of flying short hops. Train travel is up to 10 times more energy efficient.
- Limit energy use and auto emissions by walking, riding a bicycle, or using public transport.

- Shop in secondhand shops, thrift stores, or consignment shops, as well as yard and tag sales, to take advantage of gently worn goods with more life in them (or never-worn items with the price tags still on); if you don't want to wear things from strangers, organize a clothing swap with your friends.
- Stop receiving unwanted catalogs by contacting the companies to be taken off their mailing lists—or have Green Dimes (www.greendimes.com) or Catalog Choice (www.catalogchoice.org) do it for you.
- Turn off your computer when not in use and remove all screen savers, which increase electrical usage.
- Unplug any electronic devices you are not using—even when turned off, they sap small amounts of electricity.

Decorating with Green in Mind

HAVING A TRULY EARTH-FRIENDLY HOME isn't just about sealing leaks, adjusting the thermostat, or conserving water. It also involves furnishing your house and decorating the rooms with green products. To answer this need, a whole new home goods industry has arisen, so you should have no trouble finding furniture, fabrics, cushions, cabinets, paint, carpeting, paneling, flooring, countertops, tiles, and wall coverings that are all environmentally friendly.

RECYCLE, RECLAIM, REUSE

One of the easiest ways to begin making your home green is by furnishing it with antique, secondhand, and consignment store items or using family heirlooms. Or you can create your own vintage decor by repurposing old clothing and linens into pillow shams, quilts, napkins, placemats, or curtains. "Found" objects, such as old hand tools, seasoned wine crates, or a forgotten treasure from a relative's attic can also make an interesting statement in your green home.

▶ The surging demand for organic fabrics, such as cotton, bamboo, and hemp, means fewer toxins going into the ground, air, water, and food supply.

▼ This eco-friendly couch is made with a wood frame harvested from a sustainable domestic forest and cushions that incorporate recycled fiber.

BUYING TIPS

As with other products, try to shop locally for your home furnishings to eliminate the added carbon footprint of shipping. On the other hand, if items are foreign-made but support fair trade, or if the company that makes them has a good track record

Spreading the Word

In recent years, magazines such as *Vanity Fair* and *Town & Country* have devoted entire issues to green living, including green interiors. In 2008 *Country Living*'s House of the Year was a green home that incorporated many innovative, eco-friendly interior ideas.

on environmental issues, feel free to buy. Also, whenever possible, purchase items that are already in stock.

FURNITURE

When selecting upholstered furniture, choose natural fabrics that are sustainable, such as cotton, linen, silk, wool, jute, hemp, and bamboo. Also look for fabrics printed with natural inks and dyes. Polyurethane foam cushions take time to disintegrate in a landfill and are treated with chemicals, so shop for cushions made of soy foam or natural latex foam instead. Rather than throwing out a foam couch or chair, have it reupholstered in natural fabric. If you are buying new wood furniture, look for formaldehyde-free stain and low-VOC (volatile organic compound) paint. PlyBoo furniture, made from renewable bamboo, is available for living rooms, dining rooms, and bedrooms.

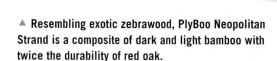

▲ Resembling exotic zebrawood, PlyBoo Neopolitan Strand is a composite of dark and light bamboo with twice the durability of red oak.

◀ Environ biocomposite—made from recycled newsprint and soy-based resin—is a healthy alternative to toxic plywoods. Varia resin, which can encase leaves and other motifs, offers a glass alternative for tabletops.

FLOORING

Opt for carpets in natural, untreated fibers, such as wool, cotton, and sisal. A home without carpeting may be healthier for anyone suffering from allergies or respiratory ailments, because rugs harbor dirt and allergens, such as dust mites and pet dander. If you choose to go carpet-free, try flooring of properly aged bamboo, reclaimed wood or cork, or linoleum.

▲ Your pets can be a key factor in what flooring you chose for your home; scratch- and stain-resistant bamboo can make an eco-friendly alternative to standard material.

◀ Made from recycled PET plastic, the kind used for soda bottles, this carpeting can be recycled again when it wears out.

◄ **A Vetrazzo countertop compares favorably with granite for strength and durability, but—composed of 85 percent recycled glass—outshines it in eco-friendliness.**

▼ **Luxurious Coyuchi sheets are made from organic cotton. If all cotton were grown organically, world insecticide usage would decrease by 25 percent.**

KITCHEN AND BATH

If you are remodeling your kitchen or bathroom, ask your builder about cabinets made of hay or certified wood. Avoid composite wood that contains formaldehyde. When it comes to green countertops, you can choose from ceramic tile made of recycled content; wood or butcher block with a Forest Stewardship Council (FSC) certification; stainless-steel counters made of recycled steel; concrete counters made with recycled aggregate and low-VOC sealers; recycled glass counters; and eco-friendly composite and recycled material counters. Some green flooring options for both kitchen and bath are unglazed ceramic or Terra Firma tile.

▲ **Made from linseed oil, cork, limestone, tree rosin, and minerals, Marmoleum natural linoleum comes in more than 150 colors.**

► **Origins (top) and Avonite, manufactured from recycled plastics, can be used for tabletops, molding, and even furniture.**

BEDDING

Not only should your bed linens be green, but your mattress should be as well. Most people don't realize that mattresses outgas various chemicals that can deprive them of restful sleep. Green linens in 100-percent cotton and silk can be ordered online from many mainstream merchandisers, who have introduced organic lines to appeal to consumer demand. A synthetic-free, cotton-covered mattress—filled with horsehair, cotton, flax, and wool—is available from the Swedish company Hästens, but at a premium price. If you're not up for the high price tag, JC Penney is partnering with Simmons Bedding to offer the "Natural Care" line of mattresses. They contain natural, biodegradable and renewable components, such as rubber tree–based latex and a layer of base foam enhanced with soy. The foundation's interior grid includes up to 80-percent recycled steel. Living Green online offers several organic mattresses, including a crib-sized model. If you do buy polyester-blend sheets or blankets, make sure you wash them several times before using them.

Beware of Greenwashing

Products that boast a few eco-friendly benefits but also harm the environment are considered "greenwashed" because the positive features have been "washed out" by the negative ones. Watch out for "green" products that are overpackaged or contain toxins.

BATH LINENS

When it comes to bath linens, look for the 100-percent organic cotton label. Living Green offers a whole line of bath products, from tub mats and bath sheets to hemp shower curtains. Anna Sova's ultra-fluffy towels, woven of certified-organic Turkish cotton, have twice the density of regular towels.

ACCESSORIES

Candles have remained a decorating staple, but many of them have wicks that give off lead when burned. Look for environmentally friendly soy candles and lead-free wicks. For wall decor and tabletop pieces, consider fair-trade handicrafts that support indigenous cultures. Let nature act as your interior decorator, and use seashells, geodes, bowls of dried flowers, river stones, or pinecones throughout your rooms.

These soy candles contain no dyes or petroleum and have natural cotton wicks. A soy candle burns cleanly, leaving no residue.

How Much Energy Use Is Too Much?

WHEN IT COMES TO ENERGY USE, the United States tops the list, far outstripping the other countries of the world. Although the United States ranks third in world population, it uses more energy than the other five most-populated countries combined, including Russia and China. Startlingly, though Americans make up 5 percent of the world's population, they consume 23 percent of its energy.

Why is it that Americans use so much energy, especially compared to other developed nations? The country's economy is partly to blame; after all, the United States does has the highest GDP (gross domestic product) in the world. By the early 2000s, America was consuming nearly 98 quadrillion British thermal units (Btu) of energy (that equates to about 1 million Btu daily for every

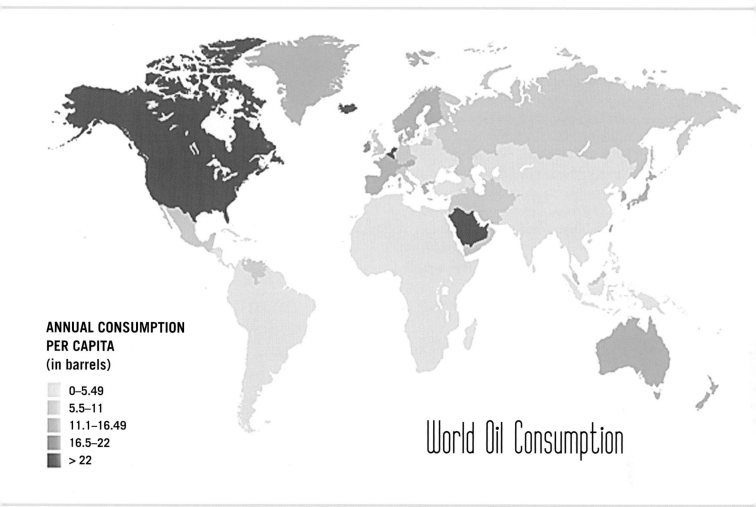

**ANNUAL CONSUMPTION
PER CAPITA
(in barrels)**

- 0–5.49
- 5.5–11
- 11.1–16.49
- 16.5–22
- > 22

World Oil Consumption

BP, "Statistical Review of World Energy," 2007

What Is a Btu?

A Btu measures the amount of energy it will take to raise the temperature of 1 pound of water by 1°F. Since water gains and increases density with an increase and decrease of temperature, this unit may vary slightly, so scientists usually use 39°F as the standard; water is at its most dense at this temperature. For those of us who aren't scientists, a Btu is about as much energy that is created when a kitchen match is lit. The Btu has become the standard for measuring heating and cooling systems in the United States. If you get a gas meter, your usage is measured in therms, one of which equals 100,000 Btu.

Btus measure heat, and watts measure electricity usage, with a single watt equivalent to 3.412 Btu. The higher the Btu of an appliance, the more powerful it is and the more energy it uses when compared to equipment with a lower Btu but the same energy-efficiency rating.

man, woman, and child). Yet in spite of economic growth of 126 percent since the early 1970s, the nation's energy usage has only increased by 30 percent. Still, experts predict a continued upswing in usage, with a 40 percent increase by 2025. Meeting this demand will mean continued reliance on foreign oil—and all the economic, environmental, and political repercussions that accompany it.

Americans are also crazy for electronic gadgets. Witness the popularity of cell phones, portable music devices and handheld computer games, and personal managers. Americans have surrounded themselves with every labor-saving device available on the market, but until recently many people didn't consider the cost to the environment.

SAVE ENERGY BY PREVENTING WASTE

Just as time is money, waste is money, too. During the past two decades, the amount of waste per person in the United States has almost doubled (from 2.7 to 4.4 pounds a day). What can be done? As simple as it seems, the most effective way to prevent waste is to not make it in the first place. Waste prevention, also called "source reduction," avoids the creation of garbage by giving new life to what was to be thrown out. Here are some tips for reducing your waste.

- Consider reusable products, rather than disposables.
- Maintain and repair durable products.
- Reuse bags, containers, and other items.
- Borrow, rent, or share rarely used items. Sell or donate goods instead of throwing them out.
- Compost yard trimmings and certain food scraps.

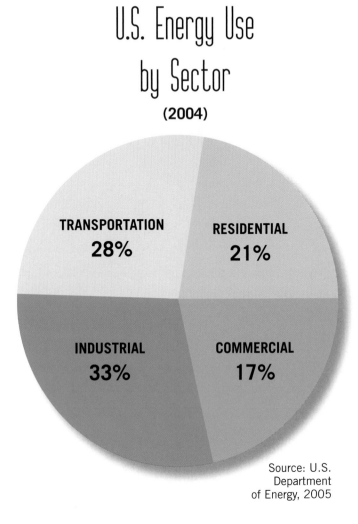

U.S. Energy Use by Sector
(2004)

TRANSPORTATION 28%

RESIDENTIAL 21%

INDUSTRIAL 33%

COMMERCIAL 17%

Source: U.S. Department of Energy, 2005

WHAT CAN YOU DO?

If you look at the pie chart that breaks down American energy use, you'll see that there are two sectors an individual can easily affect—residential, which contributes about one fifth of overall usage, and transportation, responsible for nearly one third of usage. If you curtail energy use at home and drive less, either by using mass transit or walking when possible—and encourage others to do the same—you can help to shift usage away from those areas.

Most fleece products, such as jackets, scarves, gloves, and boots, are now made from recycled plastic soda bottles.

On the Right Track

Don't throw up your hands and give up! We are making progress.

• More than 55 million tons of MSW (municipal solid waste) were source reduced—see "Waste Prevention," opposite—in the United States in 2000, the latest year for which these figures are available.

• Containers and packaging represented approximately 28 percent of the materials source reduced in 2000, in addition to nondurable goods (such as newspapers and clothing) at 17 percent, durable goods (appliances, furniture, tires) at 10 percent, and other MSW (yard trimmings, food scraps) at 45 percent.

• There are more than 6,000 reuse centers around the country, ranging from specialized programs for building materials or unneeded materials in schools to local programs such as Goodwill and the Salvation Army, according to the Reuse Development Organization.

• Since 1977, the weight of 2-liter plastic soft drink bottles has been reduced from 68 grams to 51 grams. That means that 250 million pounds of plastic per year have been kept out of the waste stream.

Doing a Home Energy Audit

By doing a home energy audit, you will be able to tell if leaky windows, doors, and vents or excess electrical use are costing you hard-earned money and wasting valuable resources. You can perform the evaluation yourself, or hire a professional home energy auditor to do it for you. A pro will probably find a greater number of waste areas than you could on your own, but you can still uncover a lot of trouble spots during your walkthrough.

DO-IT-YOURSELF AUDIT

To begin, make a checklist of potential problem areas. These should include locating air leaks, checking your insulation, inspecting your heating and cooling equipment, and checking your indoor and outdoor lighting. As you inspect each area, check it off on your list and make a note of any problems you find.

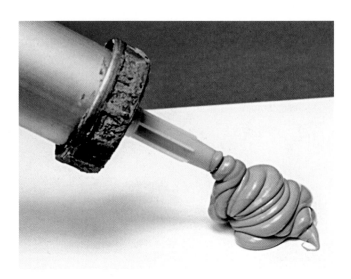

Pet doors allow air leaks, but constantly opening and closing the door plays havoc with indoor temperature control. Choose the correct door size for the size of your pet. An oversize opening will cost more and waste energy.

CHECKING FOR AIR LEAKS

Because making your home more airtight can result in a 5 to 30 percent savings per year on heating costs, this should be the first area you cover during your audit. There are two easy methods of checking for air leaks. First, close all windows and doors. Then walk through the house carrying a lit candle. Even the slightest draft near a window or door will cause the flame to waver. The other method is to wet your hand and hold it near a suspected draft. If air is flowing, your wet hand will feel cold.

Some common culprits for leaks are:

- Electrical outlets and switch plates
- Window frames
- Weather stripping around doors and bottoms of doors
- Baseboards
- Fireplace dampers
- Attic hatches
- Air conditioners
- Dryer vents
- Gaps around pipes and wires
- Mail slots and pet doors

What is R-value?

When buying insulation for your home, chose a product based on its R-value, rather than on thickness or weight. R-value ratings measure insulation's ability to resist heat flow, and the higher the R-value, the more effective the insulation.

Make sure all caulking and weather stripping have been properly applied and are in good condition. You can seal pipes with fresh caulk, or use a spray foam that hardens to form a tight seal. Check storm doors and storm windows to make sure that they fit properly and are not broken. If your windows are of single thickness with wood frames, consider upgrading to high-performance windows. Check that your attic hatch is insulated and that your attic has a vapor barrier—polyethylene sheets—under the insulation. Also make sure that the attic air vent is not covered or blocked.

CHECKING YOUR INSULATION

Over time, even a house that originally had proper insulation will start to lose heat. Especially in older houses, built when the standards were more lax, the level of insulation might no longer be adequate. Ideally, 1 inch of insulation should equal 30 inches of concrete. The only way to truly test the state of your insulation is with a thermographic inspection.

Comparing Home Insulation

R-VALUES OF COMMONLY USED HOME INSULATION PRODUCTS

(PER INCH)

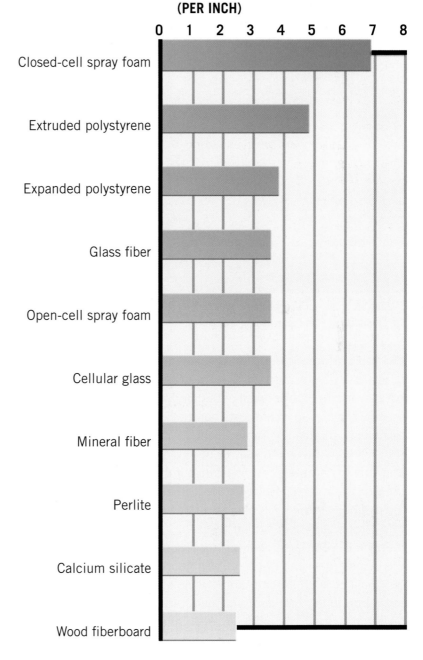

Sealing all of the duct connections with duct mastic increases the efficiency of your home heating system.

But you can do some exploring to see what sort of insulation your home has. Turn off the circuit breaker for an exterior wall outlet, and remove the cover plate. To make sure that the socket is turned off, plug in a lamp to test it. Probe inside the wall with a wooden skewer or long screwdriver. You should definitely feel resistance if the wall's interior is properly insulated. You can also make a small hole in the back of a closet or behind the refrigerator, and do a similar test.

Check in your basement for insulation under the living area—an unheated basement should be insulated with a minimum R-value of 25. The insulation in the first floor perimeter and above a heated basement should have an R-value of 19 or higher. Bear in mind that when insulation gets wet, its R-value—and its efficiency—is decreased.

INSPECTING HEATING AND COOLING EQUIPMENT

It's best to inspect your heating and cooling equipment once a year. If you find sooty streaks near duct seams, you have an air leak. Seal the seams with duct mastic. Ducts or pipes that run through unheated areas need insulation with a minimum R-value of 6. Replace all heater and air conditioner filters every two months during periods of high usage. It's also a good idea to have a professional check and clean the equipment annually. Think about replacing older units with new, energy-efficient models, especially if your state or local municipality is offering a rebate for turning in your old air conditioner

INSPECTING LIGHTING

About 10 percent of your energy bill is typically used for lighting. Check all the light fixtures in your home and yard, and wherever possible replace high-watt bulbs with 60- or 70-watt bulbs. For three-way lamps, use three-way bulbs so that you can adjust your light, and for overheads, you might install a dimmer switch for energy savings, with the added benefit of mood lighting. Consider compact fluorescent bulbs for high-use areas or for lights that remain on for long periods. For outdoor lighting, it's more economical to use motion detector lights that turn off after a few minutes. You can also illuminate walkways, driveways, and gardens with inexpensive solar-powered lights.

HIRING A PROFESSIONAL HOME ENERGY AUDITOR

A professional auditor uses a variety of techniques and equipment to gauge the energy efficiency of your home, including blower doors that measure the extent of leaks in the house's envelope and infrared cameras that can detect areas of air infiltration and missing insulation. Check with your utility company to see if it offers free or reduced-rate energy audits to its customers.

A blower door measures how airtight a house or building is, while locating air leaks. For best results, do a test both before and after you weather strip and seal, and make improvements to ensure effectiveness.

Renewable Energy

DESPITE MOST GREEN HOMEOWNERS' good intentions, they are at the mercy of the existing power companies when it comes to running their homes. Unless you plan to rely completely on alternative energy sources, the best way to offset the carbon footprint of fossil fuel combustion is by reducing your electrical usage.

THE BIG THREE

The burning of petroleum products is a leading contributor to the production of greenhouse gases. Much of the oil consumed by the United States must be shipped from foreign countries, adding to the industry's carbon footprint. Unrest in oil-rich regions has also put the country's supply lines at risk, while contributing to higher prices at the pumps.

Coal, the most abundant fossil fuel in the nation, is used to generate approximately half the electricity produced in the United States. We've got an ample supply, but it's not the best choice from an ecological standpoint—mining pollutes both land and water, and burning coal produces carbon dioxide, as well as sulfur, nitrogen oxide, and mercury. Efforts have been made by some coal plants to lessen coal pollution with scrubbers before it hits the smokestack; depending on whether low- or high-sulfur coal is used, this has resulted in anywhere from a 40- to 80-percent reduction in emissions. Although some power plants have installed scrubbers, the majority haven't, so much more needs to be done to decrease pollution.

Natural gas, found in deposits below the earth's surface, is the cleanest of the fossil fuels because its combustion releases the fewest pollutants. It is also a rich source of the hydrogen used in fuel cells. Yet, like the other fossil fuels, the supply of natural gas is finite.

NATURE'S ANSWER

Oil, coal, and natural gas are not renewable energy sources; they took millions of years to form underground and cannot be replicated. Nonetheless, a number of naturally occurring renewable energy sources make attractive alternatives to traditional fossil fuels. Once these natural resources—sunlight, wind, river water, tides, and geothermal heat—are harnessed, they can be replenished without any impact on the environment.

Your Local Green Energy Option

Can you get green energy for your home from your local power company's grid? Maybe. Green power is available in all 50 states. Some localities give you a variety of companies to choose from, while others are more limited. Although your basic energy provider stays the same, this new subcontracting of energy suppliers lets you choose where your energy dollars go. No, there's not a direct line from the green energy supplier to your home, but if the company you choose obtains all of its energy from low-impact hydroelectric and wind, then the percentage of energy you consume comes from that company. The more green energy gets bought, the more money these companies will have to create better infrastructure and reduce costs with improved efficiency. Green energy usually costs a few cents more per kilowatt-hour than conventional energy, but this might be offset by a state sales tax reduction or elimination, not to mention the benefit to the environment. Go to http://www.epa.gov/greenpower/pubs/gplocator.htm to find your local green energy provider.

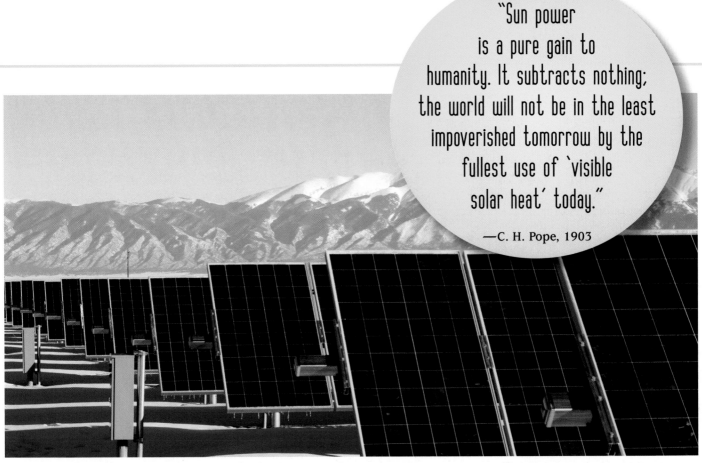

This SunEdison power plant started producing energy in December 2007. Currently one of the largest photovoltaic plants in the United States, the Alamosa Photovoltaic Plant, in the San Luis Valley of Colorado, has a locale considered ideal for solar power production.

Soon the trickle of alternatives will turn into an ocean of choices as America begins serious investigation of, and then investment in, renewable energy sources. As of 2008, however, only solar and wind technologies are practical for powering the individual home, although small-scale geothermal plants are under development.

SOLAR POWER

The sun generates power in the form of heat and light, along with secondary solar resources, such as wind and wave power. Together they account for 99.9 percent of the planet's available flow of renewable energy. Ancient Greek, Chinese, and Native American cultures all took advantage of solar power by orienting their homes toward the sun for warmth. Today solar power has a variety of applications, including heating buildings through passive solar design. Sunlight can generate electricity through photovoltaic solar cells by using concentrated solar power, and by heating trapped air that rotates turbines in a solar updraft tower. Solar-powered satellites in geosynchronous orbit can also generate electricity. Thermal panels can be used to heat water and air in the home or your backyard pool. Thermal chimneys can both heat and cool air. Skylights provide a good way to bring in light and cut energy use, but they can't be installed everywhere.

WATER POWER

The power of moving water was harnessed by early civilizations in the form of waterwheels used for grinding grain, sawing timber, and providing irrigation. During the Industrial Revolution, water was rerouted from rivers and used to spin the tur-

The RITE (Roosevelt Island Tidal Energy) Project's six turbines use the power of New York City's East River to supply electricity to a supermarket and parking garage.

bines that powered machinery in mills and factories. By the early twentieth century, large dams with hydroelectric plants were being used to generate electricity, and they currently produce 19 percent of the world's electrical power. Hydroelectric dams are also highly efficient; they can meet energy demands during peak periods and then simply store water during periods of lower demand. One objection to the construction of large-scale dams is the loss of human and animal habitats, as well as the destruction of historical sites.

Non-dam "run-of-river" projects use only part of the water flow to generate electricity. This low-impact method is environmentally friendly and helps to create domestic jobs.

TIDAL POWER

Water is roughly 800 times denser than air, so even a lapping wave can generate more power than a stiff breeze. Starting in the 1960s, France, Canada, and Russia began using tide-driven turbines to generate electricity in areas with a wide tidal range. The only drawback is that the greatest amount of power is generated only once with each tide, or every six hours. A new technology, called tidal stream power, is similar to wind turbines, drawing power from the ocean's currents. Although this technology is still unproven, the Canadian company Blue Energy has plans to begin installing "tidal fences" with vertical axis turbines in various locations around the world. The power of surface waves has the potential to produce even more electricity than tides, but this technology is quite new. In 2006, a shore-based wave power generator was constructed at Port Kembla in Australia and is expected to generate up to 500 megawatt-hours annually. The floating generator has also become a FAD, a "fish aggregating device," to the delight of local divers. In 2006, the first U.S. tidal turbines were installed by Verdant Power in New York City's East River; after a trial run of these six, plans are to increase the number to between 100 and 300, enough to power 7,000 homes.

Facts and Figures

- Only 7 percent of total United States energy consumption came from renewable sources in 2006.
- Fossil fuels are depleted at a rate that is 100,000 times faster than they are formed.
- It would be cheaper to install solar panels for the 2 billion people without access to electricity worldwide than to extend the electrical grid.
- Within 15 years, renewable energy could be generating enough electricity to power 40 million homes and offset 70 days of oil imports.

WIND POWER

Wind turbines, or wind generators, consist of high towers with rotating blades that are powered by the flow of air, converting the kinetic energy of the wind to mechanical energy, which is in turn converted to electricity. As wind flow increases, the output of the turbine rises dramatically, up to 5 megawatts, although most commercial wind turbines have a rated electrical output of 1.5 to 3 megawatts. Wind farms are typically located in areas where air currents are strong and constant, such as offshore or on hilltops. Although wind power is the fastest growing area in renewable energy technology, globally it provides less than .05 percent of energy consumed. The long-term potential of wind power is estimated at 40 times current electricity demand, but this would require enormous amounts of land devoted to wind farms. For wind power to reach its true potential, advocates will need to focus on offshore sites. There has also been some research done on airborne wind turbines, and combining wind turbines with other power sources. Some objections to harnessing wind power include the noise factor of the spinning blades and "eye pollution"—the high visibility of the towers when they line a rural hilltop.

GEOTHERMAL POWER

Deep within the earth's core lies a reservoir of untapped power—geothermal energy. Where this superheated water lies close to the planet's crust, it often rises to the surface in hot springs or gushes into the air in geysers. It is here, in countries such as Iceland, New Zealand, the Philippines, Italy, and the United States, that power plants are able to convert geothermal energy to electricity. Three types of geothermal processing plants exist—dry-steam plants take steam from ground fractures and use it to drive a turbine; flash plants absorb hot water from the ground, allow it to boil

Hawaii and Utah each have one geothermal plant, while Nevada has 15 and California boasts 33. Though the U.S. produces more electricity derived from geothermal than any other country, this accounts for only 1 percent of the total amount of the nation's output.

as it rises, and then separate the steam to run turbines; and binary plants run the hot water through heat exchangers, boiling an organic fluid that propels the turbines. In all three plants, the condensed steam and hot water are injected back into the rock to pick up more heat. Geothermal plants can be expensive to build, but their operating costs are low, a savings they can pass on in the cost of electricity.

Why Green Power?

- Domestic availability—reduces dependence on foreign imports
- Unlimited supply—won't run out as fossil fuels eventually will
- Stable price—with increased production, power will only get less expensive
- Economic growth—increases the U.S. share of the renewable market and creates jobs

Chapter 3

HUMMING ALONG

Appliances and Home Comfort Systems

SUPPLYING ENERGY TO THE average American house creates more than three tons of carbon emissions each year: that's more than twice the amount of the average car. Listen to the dead silence inside your house during a power failure, and you'll start to understand why everyday devices consume so much energy. Motors, fans, heaters, and all sorts of other electrical systems that we take for granted are humming along nonstop. Although individual appliances often don't cost very much to operate, their cumulative power draw adds up to a sizable carbon bill. Make informed choices when shopping for any of the major modern conveniences—from kitchen and laundry appliances to air-conditioning and heating equipment. By undertaking some eco-friendly home improvement, you can help the earth and save energy and money down the road.

How Much Energy Do Appliances Use?

DETERMINING HOW MUCH USING AN APPLIANCE adds to your electricity bill is pretty straightforward. To achieve the most accurate measure of usage, do the math yourself. (See "How to Calculate Electricity Usage," right.) Each appliance in your house will tell you how much power it needs, and you can decide how often and for how long to use it. Another method is to use the tables on page 49 (or other tables like it) to get a ballpark estimate of average wattage.

Of course, not all appliances use electricity or electricity alone. Multiple appliances in your house that use natural gas (or LP), such as a water heater, a furnace, or a gas stove, can make it difficult to pinpoint the energy usage of each particular appliance. With appliances that use water, namely dishwashers and clothes washers, the majority of the energy used goes toward heating the water. This heating cost is also difficult to calculate precisely, When shopping for new gas appliances, however, there is plenty of information available for comparing the efficiency rates of different products.

> "A penny saved is a penny earned."
> —Benjamin Franklin

efficiency measures are needed most. For example, if you're trying to decide whether to upgrade your refrigerator or your clothes dryer, finding the annual power draw of each will tell you which upgrade will yield greater energy savings. Understanding usage also helps in deciding where to make cutbacks. If you're like a lot of people and keep an old fridge or freezer going in the garage or basement, you can find out how much that convenience is costing you—and the environment.

HOW TO CALCULATE ELECTRICITY USAGE

Most electric appliances carry a rating tag, stamp, or badge that states the power requirements of the product. These power specs may be listed in one or more of the following measures:

- **Watts (W)**: The power used when the appliance is running.
- **Volts (V)**: The proper voltage for operating the appliance.
- **Amps or amperes (A)**: The measure of current flow or draw; for this calculation, you don't need to know the technical differences between volts and amps.

WHY MEASURE ELECTRICITY USAGE?

Knowing how much power your major appliances use can help you determine where and when

DIRECT PLUG-IN
CLASS 2 TRANSFORMER

INPUT: 120V AC 60Hz 6W
OUTPUT: 9V DC 300mA

+ —●— —

88Y3 LISTED E140898   LR89553

MODEL: 35-9-300C
EIA 363 9816 D
MADE IN CHINA

A power supply tag, stamp, or label is found on nearly all electrical appliances.

Don't Keep Your Old Fridge

Getting rid of an extra fridge or backup freezer is one of the easiest ways to take a big chunk out of your home's energy load. Most people find that with better organization—and occasional mining of unidentified parcels in the freezer—they get by just fine with one full-size refrigerator. Be sure to recycle the old unit through a reputable recycler.

LIGHTING
Averages 1,178 kilowatt-hours per year

REFRIGERATOR
Averages 1.239 kilowatt-hours per year

TRASH COMPACTOR
Averages 21 kilowatt-hours per year

DISHWASHER
Averages 591 kilowatt-hours per year

ELECTRIC RANGE
Averages 976 kilowatt-hours per year

In the United States, most appliances run on 120 volts (standard voltage). Clothes dryers, ovens, cooktops, hot-water heaters, and some other appliances typically run on 240 volts (high voltage).

To calculate daily usage, multiply an appliance's wattage rating by the number of hours you use it each day, or how long the appliance runs on its own each day. To find the monthly or annual usage, multiply your first sum by 30 or 365, respectively. For example, if your TV uses 120 watts, and it's on for 3 hours a day:

$$120 \times 3 = 360 \text{ watts/day}$$
$$360 \times 30 = 10,800 \text{ watts/month}$$
$$360 \times 365 = 131,400 \text{ watts/year}$$

If an appliance's badge gives you the amps instead of watts, multiply the amp rating by the voltage (120 in most cases) to find the wattage:

$$3 \text{ amps} \times 120 \text{ volts} = 380 \text{ watts}$$

Finally, convert to kilowatt-hours: power companies measure residential electricity usage in kilowatt-hours (kWh), or 1,000 watt-hours. A 100-watt light bulb burning for 10 hours uses 1 kWh of electricity. Your monthly utility bill should state your kWh usage for that month, as well as the price for each kWh (currently around 8 to 12 cents per kWh).

New steel is made with at least some recycled steel. Steel recycling has increased substantially in the last decade. Ninety percent of all old appliances, including old stoves and refrigerators, are now recycled.

To convert to kWh, divide the appliance usage by 1,000:

$$360 \text{ watts/day} \div 1,000 =$$
$$0.36 \text{ kWh/day (or } 131.4 \text{ kWh/year)}$$

If your electricity rate is 10 cents per kWh, your TV costs $13.14 per year to operate.

RECYCLING APPLIANCES

Old appliances don't belong in the landfill. They can be rich sources of recyclable materials, and many contain hazardous pollutants, such as ozone-depleting refrigerants and insulation, mercury, PCBs, and heavy metals. Just about all major appliances can—and should—be recycled, as should computer equipment, home electronics, old fluorescent light fixtures, and CFLs.

To learn how to recycle an old appliance, first check with your city or local recycling authority. For computers and electronics, contact the manufacturer or the store in which you bought the goods. Many sponsor convenient recycling or trade-in programs.

Resources for more info on recycling:

• **American Council for an Energy-Efficient Economy:** www.aceee.org/consumer-guide/disposal.htm
• **Earth911:** www.earth911.org/recycling
• **Energy Star:** www.recycle-myoldfridge.com

TYPICAL WATTAGE OF COMMON HOUSEHOLD APPLIANCES

Kitchen

APPLIANCE	TYPICAL WATTAGE
Barbecue grill	1,350
Blender	200–400
Broiler	1,440
Carving knife	90
Coffee maker	900–1200
Cook-top range	500
Deep-fat fryer	1,450
Dishwasher	200–2,400
Electric frying pan	1,200
Grill (sandwich)	1,160
Hot plate (single)	660
Microwave oven	750–1,100
Mixer	200
Oven (regular or self-clean)	3,750
Range	12,500
Refrigerator-freezer	240–330
Refrigerator-freezer (frost-free)	610–750
Roaster	1,330
Slow cooker or crock pot	150
Toaster	800–1,400
Toaster oven	225
Trash compactor	1,100
Waffle iron	1,120
Waste disposer	450

Laundry

APPLIANCE	TYPICAL WATTAGE
Clothes dryer	1,800–5,000
Clothes iron	1,000–1,800
Clothes washer	350–500

Heating and Cooling

APPLIANCE	TYPICAL WATTAGE
Air conditioner (window)	4,000
Fan (box)	125
Furnace (electric)	30,000
Heater (baseboard)	1,500
Heater (permanent baseboard)	1,500
Heater (portable)	1,500
Water heater (40-gallon)	4,500–5,500
Water pump (deep well)	250–1,100

Home Entertainment

APPLIANCE	TYPICAL WATTAGE
Aquarium	50–1,210
Game system	30–165
Radio (stereo)	70–400
Stereo minisystem	50
Televisions	
19"	65–110
27"	113
36"	133
53"–61" Projection	170
Flat screen	120
LCD	70
Plasma	246
TV accessories	
Analog cable box	10
DVR (or TiVo)	37
Digital cable box	26
Satellite receiver	16
VCR/DVD	17–21 / 20–25

Home Office

APPLIANCE	TYPICAL WATTAGE
Personal computer	
CPU (awake/asleep)	120/30 or less
Monitor (awake/asleep)	1,150/30 or less
Laptop	50
Inkjet printer	9
Laser printer	39
Modem	6
Wireless router	6

Personal Care

APPLIANCE	TYPICAL WATTAGE
Curling iron	400
Electric blanket (single/double)	60/100
Electric shaver	15
Electric toothbrush	250
Hair dryer	1,200–1,875
Heating pad	65

General Appliances

APPLIANCE	TYPICAL WATTAGE
Clock radio	10
Dehumidifier	785
Fans	
Ceiling	65–175
Window	55–250
Furnace	750
Whole house	240–750
Heater (portable)	750–1,500
Vacuum cleaner	1,000–1,440

Source: U.S. Department of Energy

Energy Star and the EnergyGuide Label

WHEN SHOPPING FOR EFFICIENT APPLIANCES, look for the Energy Star logo and EnergyGuide label. Why? Because at a glance, you can tell which products meet basic efficiency standards and how each model compares in efficiency to its peers.

ENERGY STAR

The Energy Star logo is the little blue emblem you see attached to all sorts of household products—from refrigerators and computer printers to windows and home heating systems. Any product carrying the label meets the minimum efficiency standards of the Energy Star program. Energy Star products typically exceed federal minimum efficiency standards and are among the top 25 percent most efficient products in a given category.

The Energy Star program was started in 1992 by the U.S. Environmental Protection Agency (EPA) in an effort to identify and promote energy-efficient products in the marketplace. Participation in the program was, and is, voluntary, but the idea has certainly caught on. Today Energy Star boasts more than 50 product categories and includes a program that awards Energy Star status to highly efficient homes and commercial buildings.

The Energy Star Web site (www.energystar.gov) is loaded with information to teach consumers about energy-efficient appliances and other products, along with tips, calculators, and links aimed at helping you save energy throughout your home. You can also find lists of Energy Star–qualified products by category.

Unlike the EnergyGuide label, Energy Star qualification doesn't quantify performance, so it's useful for comparison purposes only in that you can quickly rule out models that aren't Energy Star. You can, however, find the qualification standards for specific appliance types on the Energy Star Web site. It's important to note that Energy Star qualification represents a range, and that some Energy Star products may be significantly more efficient than similar qualifying products.

ENERGYGUIDE LABEL

The EnergyGuide label is the big, yellow-and-black sticker found on many types of major appliances, such as refrigerators, washers, dryers, and heating and cooling equipment. Cooking appliances currently are not labeled. The EnergyGuide label, required by law and enforced by the Federal Trade Commission, provides consumers with three important criteria about a given product:

1. How much energy it uses.
2. How its energy use compares to other models in its category.
3. What it costs, on average, to operate the appliance per year.

From insulation to decorative lighting to battery chargers, products that get an Energy Star rating must conform to strict guidelines.

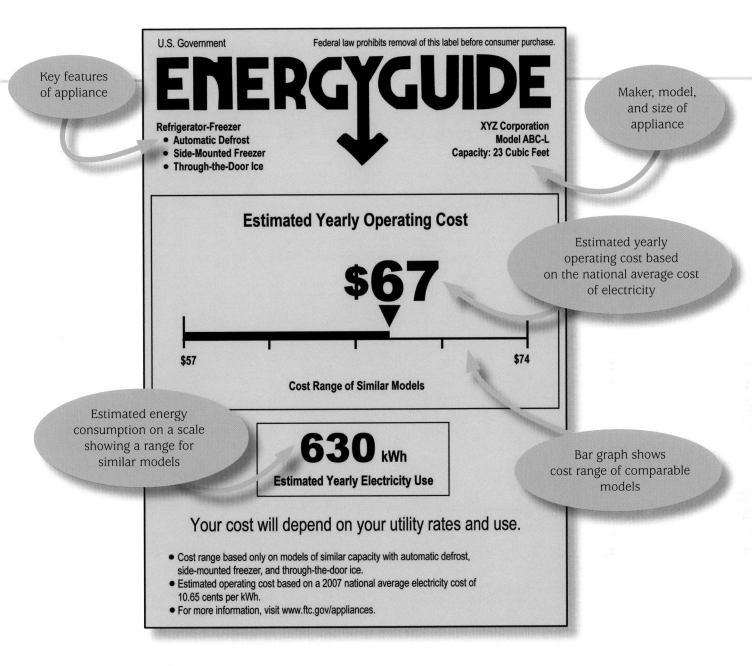

The EnergyGuide label also includes the manufacturer, model number, and a list of basic descriptive features for the product.

The bar scale (with arrow) in the center of the label provides a graphic representation of the efficiency comparison feature. The farther to your left the arrow is, the more efficient, relatively, the appliance model is. The energy cost feature is also an accurate measure for comparison; however, because this number is based on nationally averaged utility rates and appliance usage, depending on where you live, your actual costs may vary significantly from the listed estimate.

You can easily see how Energy Star and the EnergyGuide label help to streamline your shopping. If you're looking for energy-wise appliances, don't waste your time with products that aren't Energy Star (providing the product category is part of Energy Star; not all are). From there you can narrow your search to products that meet your own performance goals, using the EnergyGuide labels for easy reference.

Kitchen Appliances

Updating your kitchen with new Energy Star appliances adds value to your home and lowers your energy bills.

YOU'VE PROBABLY HEARD IT BEFORE: Kitchens use the most energy of any room in the house. That's not surprising when you consider that the refrigerator, the largest home appliance, runs 24/7, dutifully maintaining frigid temperatures in all seasons. Add to that the energy that goes into cooking and dish washing, and it's easy to see how kitchen appliances account for more than a quarter of the total electricity use in the average home. Needless to say, the kitchen is one of the best places to start making efficiency upgrades.

REFRIGERATORS

In terms of energy use, refrigerators have made impressive strides over the past few decades. Many of today's models use less than a third of the electricity of those available in the mid-1970s. And new Energy Star models are twice as efficient as standard models from just 15 years ago (they're also 20 percent more efficient than the current federal standard). These numbers are significant, because the fridge is the biggest single electricity user in most homes, accounting for around 15 percent of a homeowner's annual electricity bill.

To find out how much power you can save by replacing your old fridge, calculate its usage and compare that figure to new Energy Star models that meet your needs. Ready to go refrigerator shopping? Consider these factors before making a decision:

Freezer location/configuration: Top-freezer and bottom-freezer models are 10 to 30 percent more efficient than side-by-side freezer models.

Size: Get the size fridge that you really need. Over-sizing is clearly wasteful, but under-sizing may mean extra trips to the store, or it might tempt you to buy a second refrigerator.

Power-save switch: In most cases, this switch allows you to shut off the anticondensation feature (a heater that warms up the outer shell of the fridge; go figure).

Ice-making and water-dispensing features: Are these small conveniences really worth it? Automatic icemakers and through-the-door ice and water dispensers come with a price of 10 to 20 percent greater energy consumption.

OUT WITH THE OLD

It can't be said enough: don't keep your old fridge in use! If you really need the extra space, buy a larger energy-efficient model that fulfills your family's freezing and refrigerating requirements or even an Energy Star minifridge for backup storage. Think about the long-term energy savings: you could replace every electric appliance in your house with the most efficient model available and it probably wouldn't offset the power use of one old fridge running around the clock.

Keeping a fridge that is more than 10 years old may be costing you upward of $100 a year in electricity versus a new one.

Do you really need an in-door ice cube dispenser? It will require running a water line and increase energy consumption.

COOKING APPLIANCES

All together, the major cooking appliances account for about a quarter of the typical kitchen's electricity consumption, or roughly 7 percent of total household usage. When you divide that up among the different appliances—cooktop, oven, microwave, toaster oven, coffee maker, and so on—you end up with fairly insignificant opportunities for energy savings with this group of products. In fact, your cooking habits are likely to have a larger impact on energy usage than the appliances themselves.

That said, there are differences of energy consumption among products, fuel types, and technologies, and it makes sense to consider efficiency, along with performance factors, when shopping for new cooking appliances, especially because some of these products can last for decades. Here's a brief overview of the current popular options.

Cooktop (or range top)

The first question to answer when shopping for a cooktop is, as ever before, gas or electric? Serious cooks still prefer gas for the better heat control, while other folks want electric for the sleek look or the easy-to-clean surfaces (or simply they don't want to spring for a gas hookup when their kitchen

Blue Flames Are True

If you use a gas cooktop, make sure the burner flames are blue, which means that the gas is burning completely. A yellow flame indicates poor combustion and thus more indoor air pollution; time to call in a service pro.

Electric burners cool off more slowly than gas ones, so you can turn off an electric burner several minutes before the dish in your pot is done to achieve the same results as you would with gas.

is already wired for electric). The choice is up to you. But if you like cooking with gas, think twice about switching to electric based on the perceived energy savings alone.

Cooktops are rated for energy efficiency based on how well the heat energy is transferred from the source (the burner) to the pan. Standard electric cooktops, including old-fashioned coils, radiant ceramic ("glass top"), and halogen models offer about 68 to 78 percent efficiency. Induction cooktops, which use electromagnetism to heat pans, are about 80 to 84 percent efficient. By comparison, new gas cooktops are only about 40 percent efficient, and older models—with a constantly burning pilot light instead of electronic ignition—are only about 15 percent efficient. Electronic ignition is a no-brainer; it saves energy and reduces indoor air pollution.

Electricity efficiency isn't so simple, however, when it comes to cooking. Gas is a primary fuel source for heat, and electricity is a secondary source, so gas is a much more efficient fuel for cooking in terms of carbon emissions. Here's why: for every 1 kWh of electricity available for

Energy-Wise Kitchen Tips

Refrigeration
- Leave room for air circulation around the refrigerator's coils, and clean the coils periodically.
- Keep the fridge out of direct sunlight and away from heat sources (oven, cooktop, and the like).
- Cover food and liquid containers to prevent evaporation and condensation; they make the fridge work harder.
- Set the fridge at 36°–38°F and the freezer at 0°–3°F. These are the proper settings, and there's no need to go lower.
- Keep your freezer full but not stuffed: a full stock of frozen items helps balance the temperature to minimize on/off cycling. Overfilling restricts air circulation and reduces efficiency. Add containers of water to a sparsely filled freezer to improve efficiency.

Cooking
- Use the smallest and/or fastest appliance for the job you need to do.
- Match the pan size to the burner on electric cooktops. Pans should have flat bottoms (or slightly concave) for maximum heat transfer.
- Keep appliances clean—dirty burner pans and oven compartments (including microwaves) reduce efficiency.
- Preheat ovens only when necessary.
- Don't open oven doors more than you have to.

use in your house, on average 3 kWh of energy was consumed at the power plant. Waste heat (from burning coal, in most cases) and the transmission of power from the plant to your home accounts for the lost 2 kWh. Gas, on the other hand, is converted to heat right at your stove. When comparing natural gas to coal-produced electricity, heating a pot of water with electricity has been shown to result in carbon emissions about three and a half times greater than heating the same amount of water with gas.

Kitchen Ventilation

Along with cooking comes the matter of clearing the air in the kitchen. Just some basic advice here: overhead vent hoods are more effective and more energy-efficient than downdraft fans that pull air down into the center of a cooktop or into a pop-up vent at the back. Hoods are better because they work with nature—hot air rises—and they need less fan power to do the job. Any type of ventilation

Overhead stove hoods with exhaust fans do the best job of clearing the air. All exhaust fans are most effective when fresh outdoor air is allowed into the house, so open a window to improve ventilation.

system must also be ducted to the outdoors (never the attic) to be effective.

Ovens

Fuel type and performance in standard ovens are subject to less debate than in cooktops, but it pays to shop carefully for a product that suits the kind of cooking you do most. As with cooktops, electric ovens are rated with higher efficiency than gas, but you run into the same carbon quandary with electricity production. If you're considering a gas oven, find out how much electricity it uses when running, since most include an electric igniter bar that stays on whenever the gas is going. This can add up to a fair amount of power consumption, in addition to the gas usage.

Self-cleaning ovens of both types generally are more efficient than non-self-cleaning models, because the former are better insulated. If you

Microwaves heat food in far less time than conventional ovens. In some cases, microwaving vegetables will help them retain greater nutritional value than other lengthier methods, such as boiling.

tend to check on your food frequently, choose an oven with a window in the door. Each time you open an oven's door you lose about 20 percent of its stored heat.

Convection ovens typically are about 20 percent more efficient than standard ovens. Convection ovens have fans that circulate the hot air throughout the oven compartment, resulting in more even heating and reduced cooking times and/or lower required temperatures. Some ovens combine conventional heating with microwave technology for multiple cooking options in one appliance.

In practical use, microwave ovens are far more efficient than conventional ovens because they cook so much faster and never need to preheat. Most standard microwaves on the market offer comparable energy efficiency. Their smaller compartments also make toaster ovens more energy-wise than their full-size counterparts. And what discussion of cooking appliances would be complete without a nod to the homemaker's trusty friend, the crock-style slow cooker? It's one of the most energy-efficient ways to cook.

An old standby, the crock-style slow cooker can prepare a variety of foods. The heat from the pot, the extended cooking time, and the steam in the sealed container eliminate any bacteria.

DISHWASHERS

The dishwasher is a truly win-win appliance: it's relatively inexpensive, it saves countless hours of time, and on average, it uses less energy and water than washing dishes by hand. Today's dishwashers work so well that rinsing dishes has become a thing of the past. In fact, it's a good ecological practice not to rinse—just scrape off the solids and go right to the dishwasher; only really stubborn bits need pre-rinsing in the sink.

Most of the energy used by dishwashers goes toward heating the water—both at your home's water heater and in the dishwasher itself. The most efficient models therefore tend to use the least amount of water. Once you've settled on the size and type of dishwasher you want, compare models based on their electricity and water usage, as well as conservation settings. Energy Star dishwashers use at least 41 percent less energy than comparable standard models.

Here are some features to consider when shopping for a new dishwasher:

No-heat dry option: This saves energy by air-drying the dishes with a circulating fan rather than baking them dry with an internal heating element.

Size: Choose the right size for your everyday needs. Keep in mind that dish washing is most efficient with full loads, so it makes sense to wait until the machine is full before running it. If the model is too big, you might have to wait several days. If it's too small, you might end up running a lot more loads to keep up with your family's needs, thus negating the energy savings of a smaller unit.

Cycle settings: Depending on your usage, you might save resources using cycle options such as "light wash," "soil sensing," and "rinse only." Some models also let you wash items in the upper rack only, say for a quick cleansing of dirty glasses. Before purchasing a particular model, look through the product literature for specifications on water use and cycle times to determine how much you're really saving with alternative settings.

Water heaters: Many dishwashers have internal heaters to bring the water temperature up to 140° or 145°F for the wash cycle. This feature uses a fair amount of electricity, but it can help some households save significantly elsewhere. If you keep your water heater turned up higher than 120°F (the standard setting) to supply your dishwasher with hotter water, you can just let the dishwasher do the heating. This way, you're raising the temperature of only 10 or fewer gallons of water for each dishwasher load instead of the 40 to 70 gallons in your hot water tank, 24 hours a day.

Energy-wise Dish Washing

- Run full loads.
- Use the "no-heat dry" setting whenever practical.
- Skip the "prerinse" cycle.
- Use "high-temp" or "sanitize" cycles only when absolutely necessary.
- Insulate the hot water supply pipe between the dishwasher and hot water heater.
- Run the dishwasher during off-peak utility hours.

automatically set the water level based on how much clothing you throw in. Others have several load-size options that you select manually. Make sure that your new washer has either type of water-level control.

Water temperature is also directly linked to energy use. A cold wash with cold rinse uses 5 to 10 times less energy than a hot-wash / warm-rinse load. Any quality washing machine will come with water temperature options, but it's up to you to use them judiciously. Experiment with different wash temperatures to determine when you really need hot or warm water; most loads do fine with a cold wash. For rinsing, there's no reason to use anything but cold water.

Finally, spin speed is an energy factor because it relates directly to drying time. The faster the washer spins, the drier your clothes come out from the wash, and the less time they have to spend in the dryer. It takes a lot less energy to remove water with spinning than with heated drying.

CLOTHES DRYERS

The differences in energy efficiency among new clothes dryers is small enough that Energy Star doesn't rate them. And both gas and electric models offer similar performance. But if you're looking for a new dryer, choose a model with an automatic shutoff feature in addition to standard timer controls. Automatic shutoff senses how dry the clothes are and ends the drying when they're ready. This saves energy over timed drying because most people tend to set their timers for longer than necessary. Better shutoff mechanisms respond to humidity levels in the dryer as opposed to simple temperature readings.

Eco-friendly Fabric Softener

You can get the same results as dryer sheets and liquid fabric softeners without all the chemical additives. A pair of readily available, reusable nubby "dryer balls" tumbling around your dryer make laundry just as soft and fluffy as commercially prepared products. This is accomplished with less stress on your clothing, in addition to making drying cycles shorter.

Tips for Energy-Efficient Drying

Here are a few ways to save energy regardless of what kind of dryer you have:

- Clean the lint trap before each use.
- Make sure the dryer is well ventilated, with the shortest, straightest run of vent duct possible. Rigid metal duct is more efficient and safer than flexible plastic duct.
- Install an air-sealed vent cap on the outdoor end of the dryer duct to prevent cold air from entering the house through the vent.
- Dry by fabric type; don't mix heavy cotton towels with lightweight synthetics, for example, because their drying times vary so widely.
- Run loads in close succession to take advantage of the dryer's stored heat from the preceding load.

Nature's Clothes Dryer

The best way to save energy in the laundry room is with a highly efficient, totally free solar- and wind-powered drying system: a clothesline.

Beware the Energy Parasites

WHILE YOU SLEEP AT NIGHT, when all is dark and calm, the energy parasites are at work, silently sucking the lifeblood from your electrical system. Known as phantom loads or power vampires, these tiny ghouls reside in dozens of electric devices around the home: battery chargers, digital clocks, TVs, stereos, computer hardware, and most things that work by remote control. Without you knowing it, phantom loads run continuously, even when their host device is switched to OFF.

Although each energy vampire may survive on only a few watts of electricity, there are so many these days that together they consume nearly 1,200 kWh per year in the average home, at an annual cost of $102. And because they're made to run around the clock, there's only one way to stop them: pulling the plug.

For example, when you're done charging your cell phone or cordless tool, don't leave the charger plugged in. At the end of each workday, hit the power switch on your printer

When you are not using your home computer and its many peripherals, a quick flip of the power strip's switch from ON to OFF can save energy.

instead of leaving it in standby mode. Better yet, anywhere you have multiple vampires in a group, such as a stereo system or home office, plug everything into a power strip, and hit the master switch when the devices aren't in use. Plugging your TV, DVD player, cable box, and home theater system into a power strip or two lets you put a half dozen vampires to rest instantly.

Look for these common clues to find and snuff out other energy parasites in your home:

- Any power cord with a "brick" or "cube" at the plug end; these are low-voltage transformers that use power even when they're not charging or powering something
- Devices that stay warm long after being turned off
- "Standby" mode on any electronic appliance
- Electronic timers and integral clocks
- Any device that can be turned on by remote control
- Low-power modes, such as "sleep" mode on a personal computer

Recharge your own batteries and reduce energy consumption slightly by turning off the alarm clock on weekend mornings.

▲ Instead of numerous remotes, try a universal one to control your cable, TV, DVD player, and any other audio equipment.

▶ A UK company has come up with an adapter that detects when an appliance, such as a cell phone, mp3 player, or laptop recharger, switches into standby mode. The special adapter then cuts off power to the device, saving electricity and money.

Don't get carried away! For obvious reasons, some devices with phantom loads, such as answering machines, motion detectors, doorbells, and security systems, are useless if not plugged in. Programmable devices can be a real pain to reprogram if you cut their power. But with so many other of these power suckers, a simple change in habits and a few dollars spent on some power strips can help you sleep better at night, knowing that these tiny parasites are resting, too.

Green Lighting

IF ALL OF THE LIGHTING in the average American house accounts for only 5 to 10 percent of homeowners' annual electricity bills, why are new fluorescent lightbulbs the most widely advertised and recommended for green improvement? The answer is simple: next to turning off the lights when you leave the room, switching from standard incandescent lightbulbs to CFLs is the easiest way to make significant reductions in the nation's energy use. It's as easy as, well, screwing in a lightbulb.

CFLs produce 75 percent less heat than incandescents, meaning lower energy costs for cooling.

EVERYTHING YOU NEED TO KNOW ABOUT CFLS

Thanks to all the public awareness messaging, most people know what CFLs are. Far fewer, however, know how to choose the right CFL products for their needs. Just in case you're still in the dark: CFLs are compact fluorescent lamps (lamp is the industry's term for lightbulbs) that are made to replace standard incandescent bulbs in most household fixtures. CFLs are better than incandescents because they are three to four more energy-efficient and last seven to ten times longer, on average.

Wattage

Now, back to choosing the right products. Any well-stocked home center or hardware store should have a CFL to replace any type of incandescent bulb, from standard bulbs to flame-shaped decorative bulbs to indoor and outdoor spots and floods. Once you find the right type of lamp, check the packaging for the equivalent wattage: for example, a 20-watt CFL provides the same light output as a 75-watt incandescent (thus the energy savings).

Light Quality

Next, read the product labels to find the right quality of light. This is expressed in two numerical values: the color rendering index (CRI) and the correlated color temperature (CCT). The CRI number tells you how realistic colors will look under the light. The higher the CRI, the better. Incandescents have a CRI of 100, which means colors look pretty much as they do under daylight. CFLs aren't quite

as high; look for products with a CRI of 85 or higher for the best available color rendering.

The CCT, or color temperature, indicates how "warm" or "cool" a light source is. This is measured in degrees kelvin (K). CFLs come in four temperature ranges: 2700°K, 3000°K, 3500°K, and 4100°K. Lights at the low end of the scale are warmer, softer, and more yellow. Lights at the high end are cool and bright white. For most fluorescent products, the closest match to incandescent light is

Take a CFL Test-drive

Before investing in mega-packs of CFLs, try a few different products—with different color temperatures (CCT)—to assess their light quality in various fixtures in your home. Once you find the range you like best, you can buy in bulk to save money.

3000°K, which is best for general indoor ambient lighting. Lights at 4100°K are "daylight" bright and are better suited to task lighting and workrooms, such as a garage or laundry room.

LINEAR "TUBE" FLUORESCENTS

Tube fluorescent no longer has to mean the buzzing, flickering lights that cast a ghostly, bluish glow in office buildings and basements. Today's linear fixtures use silent electronic ballasts (no buzzing) with instant startup (no flickering), and the lamps are available with 70 to 90 CRI and the same range of color temperatures as CFLs. The most energy-efficient lamps are the thin T-5 and T-8 types (T-12 lamps are the larger tubes that you still buy for older utility-type fixtures). Low-profile linear fixtures with T-5 lamps can protrude just 1 inch and are ideal for under-cabinet kitchen lighting.

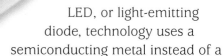

OTHER ENERGY-EFFICIENT LIGHTING OPTIONS

In addition to fluorescents, a few other lighting technologies are becoming increasingly available to consumers, namely LED, halogen, and xenon. Of the three, LED is the clear front-runner in terms of efficiency and versatility.

Replacing incandescent lamps with halogen task lighting, although not as efficient as CFLS, will still reduce energy costs.

LED, or light-emitting diode, technology uses a semiconducting metal instead of a filament (incandescent) or gas (fluorescent) to produce light. This makes the lights durable and long-lasting—up to 100,000 hours. Unlike fluorescents, which cast light in all directions, LEDs send a focused beam of light, making them ideal for bright, white task and accent lighting.

Comparing the efficiency of similar task lights, such as under-cabinet fixtures in the kitchen or stand-alone desk lamps in the den, LED produces about 40 lumens per watt (or lpw, the official measure of a light's energy efficiency), halogen produces about 20 lpw, and xenon about 15 lpw. A fluorescent T-5 lamp produces about 50 lpw.

LIGHTING Q&A

CFLs are so expensive compared with regular lightbulbs. How long does it take for CFLs to pay off?

At average electricity rates, a CFL will likely pay for itself and more in the first year of use. This table (page 69) shows the cost savings of using a 20-watt CFL (purchased for $4; many are cheaper than that) in place of a 75-watt incandescent bulb (at 50¢ each, you'd have to buy more than 10 bulbs to match the lifetime of the one CFL).

CFL SAVINGS

HOURS OF OPERATION	1ST-YEAR SAVINGS	3RD-YEAR SAVINGS	10TH-YEAR SAVINGS
2 hours per day	$0.31	$8.94	$39.14
4 hours per day	$4.63	$21.89	$78.29
8 hours per day	$13.26	$43.77	$156.07

Source: American Council for an Energy-Efficient Economy

Can lightbulbs really make a big difference for the environment?

Much bigger than most people would expect. According to the Energy Star Web site: "If every American home replaced their five most frequently used light fixtures or the bulbs in them with ones that have earned the ENERGY STAR, we would save close to $8 billion each year in energy costs, and together we would prevent the greenhouse gases equivalent to the emissions from nearly 10 million cars."

Why are some of the CFLs in my house not as bright as the incandescent bulbs that they replaced?

If the CFLs have the proper equivalent wattage to the old bulbs, their true light output (measured in lumens) should be the same. You may, however, want to try CFLs with a higher color temperature (CCT) for "whiter" light that often appears to be brighter.

Do I need special fixtures to use CFLs?

No. A standard CFL has an integral ballast (the large, plastic base connected to the bulb) and is made for use with standard light fixtures. You can also buy fixtures made for CFLs, which have their own long-lasting ballasts built into the fixture. For these, use CFLs without ballasts. Many dedicated compact fluorescent fixtures include dimming or multilevel capability.

Can I use fluorescent lighting outdoors?

Yes. Just look for CFLs rated for outdoor use. Depending on the application, you might also consider high-pressure sodium or metal halide lights, both of which are energy-efficient and commonly used for illuminating sport courts and swimming pools. For low-level landscape lighting, self-contained solar fixtures offer free energy and easy installation.

Do CFLs work with dimmers?

Standard CFLs do not, but there are many CFLs made specifically for use with dimmers; check the product labeling.

Is it true that fluorescent lights contain mercury?

Both CFLs and fluorescent tube lamps contain small amounts of mercury inside the glass tubing. CFLs contain about 4 milligrams, while a 4-foot tube lamp contains about 40 mg. When compared with the 3,000 milligrams in the typical old-fashioned wall thermostat, the mercury levels in fluorescent lamps are quite small. Nonetheless, it is hazardous waste and must be dealt with accordingly. Recycle all unbroken CFLs and fluorescent tubes through a local recycler. (For more information, visit www.epa.gov/bulbrecycling or www.earth911.org.) If a CFL or fluorescent tube breaks in your home, follow the EPA's cleaning and disposal recommendations, which you can find online at www.epa.gov/mercury/spills/index.htm.

Are low-voltage lights energy efficient?

Not so much. Many low-voltage lights use halogen bulbs, which are high-intensity incandescents. That's why they get so hot and why they're not very efficient. For focused task lighting, LED fixtures are an energy-efficient alternative to halogen.

Heating Clean and Green

IN MOST AREAS OF THE COUNTRY, heating systems are the biggest energy users in the house, accounting for 35 to 50 percent of the average annual energy bill. When combined with hot water—the biggest energy user after space heating and cooling—heating is clearly a prime target for energy savings and green upgrades.

Having the right heating equipment certainly can make a difference in your home's energy use and carbon footprint, but creating heat efficiently is only half the battle. The other challenges lie in keeping the heat indoors and the cold out—with conservation measures such as insulating, sealing air leaks, capturing solar heat, and improving window performance.

Following is an overview of the main types of heating systems, along with tips and considerations for choosing high-efficiency products. Keep in mind that heating efficiency involves several factors, including the system's design and controls and the home's thermal performance, in addition to the heating equipment itself. Before investing in major changes or upgrades, consult a home energy auditor and/or an HVAC (heating, ventilation, and air conditioning) specialist for guidance.

SOLAR SPACE HEATING

There are two ways to heat your house with solar energy. Passive solar is the age-old practice of letting sun in through the windows and, preferably, storing it in high-mass flooring and wall materials. Active solar involves solar collectors much like those used for hot water heating. Typically, the heat generated is used to supplement hydronic or forced-air heating systems. Because solar energy is totally cost-free and emissions-free, solar space heating is potentially the cleanest, greenest way to heat your home.

FURNACE SYSTEMS

Forced-air systems supplied by a natural gas or fuel oil furnace are the most common types of heating systems in the United States. Inefficiencies with these occur in the furnace itself and in the air-distribution system. To save energy with an existing system, make sure all air ducts are properly sealed with duct mastic or UL-181b certified duct tape (regular duct tape is, ironically, a poor material for sealing ducts). Insulate all hot-air supply ducts that run through unheated areas, such as a crawlspace (R-8 insulation is recommended for cold climates) to reduce heat losses through the ducts. Also, have the entire system tuned and calibrated periodically by an HVAC contractor for optimal performance.

If you're looking to buy a new furnace, limit your search to Energy Star models for either gas or oil-burning units, or look for a gas furnace with a Tier 2 or Tier 3 rating from CEE (Consortium for Energy Efficiency; www.cee1.org). Energy efficiency in a furnace is stated in its AFUE rating, which takes into account actual operating conditions and not just peak operating performance. Most high-efficiency units (AFUE or 90 percent and up for gas; 83 percent and up for oil) are condensing-type, meaning they recapture heat from the burners' exhaust to boost efficiency. Another feature to look for is sealed combustion. This uses outdoor air for combustion drawn through a sealed vent pipe, so there's no mingling of indoor air and poisonous combustion air.

BOILER SYSTEMS

Water-based, or hydronic, heating systems heat water in a gas or oil-fired boiler and circulate it through radiators, baseboard convection units, or in-floor tubing. Rooms are heated either through natural air convection or, in the case of in-floor systems, by heat radiating up through the flooring. In-floor heating works particularly well with high-mass flooring, such as concrete, stone, and tile, because these materials can absorb a lot of solar heat during the day and release it at night, thus boosting the efficiency of the system. In some well-insulated homes, a high-efficiency hot water heater feeds the radiant systems, eliminating the need for a boiler.

Like furnaces, new high-efficiency boilers may use condensing technology to recapture heat energy from the burners' exhaust. Sealed combustion is also available. Boilers meeting Energy Star standards offer at least 85 percent AFUE ratings, compared to about 80 percent for conventional

Many municipalities provide tax incentives for both active and passive space and water heating, and installation of photovoltaic cells.

new models. If you live in an old house with a two-pipe steam-heating system, it may be cost-effective to switch to a contemporary hot-water system; consult a qualified HVAC specialist.

HEAT PUMPS

Heat pumps provide both heating and cooling, and they come in two main types: air-source and ground-source (also known as geothermal). Both types use water or antifreeze circulated through tubing to draw heat or cold from the outdoors and transfer it to the home system via a heat exchanger. In winter, the tubing extracts heat from the air or ground and brings it into the house. In summer, the flow of circulating liquid is reversed, and the tubing pulls heat from the house and dumps it into the air or ground. Inside the house, the heat or cold typically is distributed by an air-handling system.

Air-source heat pumps use an outdoor unit, somewhat like a central air conditioner. These are most efficient in mild climates with long cooling seasons. Geothermal systems involve long loops of tubing either buried in shallow trenches or in deep, vertical holes in the ground (or they can run through a body of water located on the property). The tubing uses the earth, which stays at a nearly constant temperature of around 55°F, to extract or dump heat depending on the season. Geothermal systems are up to 45 percent more efficient than air-source heat pumps. They are quite expensive to install but offer very low operating costs and energy use, making them one of the greenest choices for those building new, sustainable homes.

WOOD STOVES AND FIREPLACES

High-efficiency wood-burning stoves and some gas fireplaces can be fairly green options for supplemental space heating or even as the sole heat sources for very small homes. The operative term here is "high-efficiency," meaning heating

◀ With the look of a traditional wood-burning stove, an electric pellet stove burns small pieces of recycled sawdust that have been compressed into pellets.

▼ Wood pellet fuel is clean burning and energy efficient. It is also cheap and produces very little waste.

What Is Radiant Heating?

Radiant heating systems supply heat directly to a house's floor or panels in the walls or the ceiling.

This kind of heating is more efficient than baseboard heating and usually more efficient than forced-air heating because no energy is lost through ducts. The lack of ducts also can keep allergens from blowing around. Hydronic (liquid-based) systems don't use much electricity, so they work well for homes off the power grid or in areas with high electricity prices. Hydronic systems can also be heated with a wide variety of energy sources, including standard gas- or oil-fired boilers, wood-fired boilers, solar water heaters, or a combination of options. They don't take up interior wall space with ductwork and run quietly (no clanking).

Wall- and ceiling-mounted radiant panels are usually made of aluminum and can be heated with either electricity or tubing that carries hot water. The majority of radiant panels for homes are electrically heated.

Unlike other types of radiant heating systems, radiant panels have very low heat capacity, so you can increase the temperature setting and reach a comfortable level within minutes. Because the panels can be individually controlled for each room, the quick response feature may save money and energy, especially for infrequently used spaces. Of course, as with any system, the thermostat must be maintained at a minimum temperature that will prevent pipes from freezing.

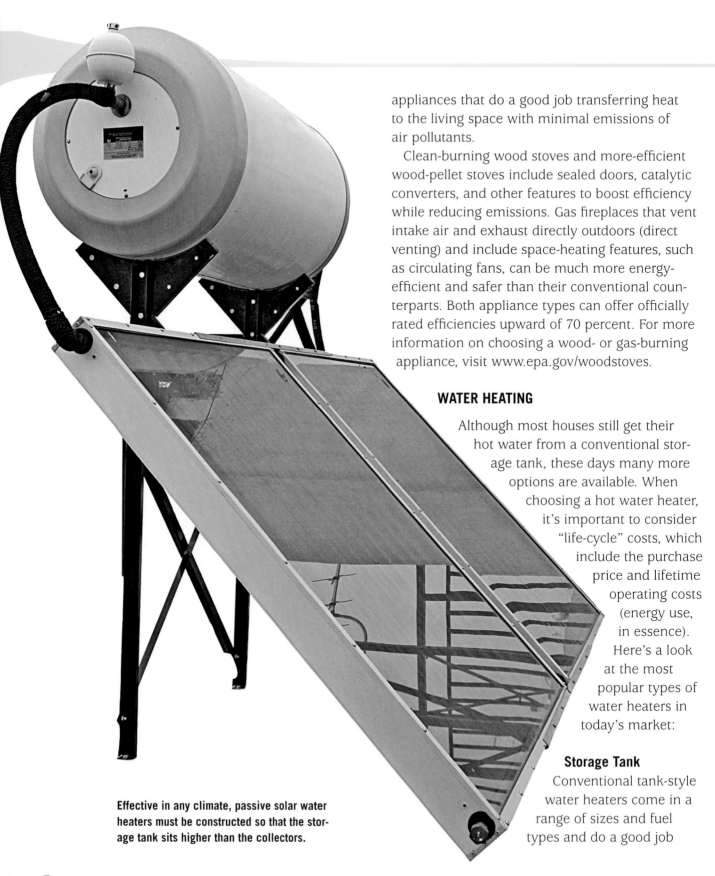

appliances that do a good job transferring heat to the living space with minimal emissions of air pollutants.

Clean-burning wood stoves and more-efficient wood-pellet stoves include sealed doors, catalytic converters, and other features to boost efficiency while reducing emissions. Gas fireplaces that vent intake air and exhaust directly outdoors (direct venting) and include space-heating features, such as circulating fans, can be much more energy-efficient and safer than their conventional counterparts. Both appliance types can offer officially rated efficiencies upward of 70 percent. For more information on choosing a wood- or gas-burning appliance, visit www.epa.gov/woodstoves.

WATER HEATING

Although most houses still get their hot water from a conventional storage tank, these days many more options are available. When choosing a hot water heater, it's important to consider "life-cycle" costs, which include the purchase price and lifetime operating costs (energy use, in essence). Here's a look at the most popular types of water heaters in today's market:

Storage Tank
Conventional tank-style water heaters come in a range of sizes and fuel types and do a good job

Effective in any climate, passive solar water heaters must be constructed so that the storage tank sits higher than the collectors.

supplying a lot of hot water during peak usage times. In terms of efficiency, their main drawback is that the water loses heat as it sits in the tank, known as "standby loss." The most efficient conventional gas-fired models today offer an energy factor (EF) of 0.65 and higher, and some include sealed combustion for greater efficiency and improved indoor air quality. Generally, electric tank water heaters are not energy efficient.

Tankless or On-demand

Tankless water heaters are compact gas or electric units that heat water only as it's called for at the tap, eliminating the standby heat losses that come with tank-style heaters. Tankless units cost more than tank heaters but can be 15 to 20 percent more energy efficient. They also last longer than tank units, so their potential life-cycle costs can be significantly lower. When considering a tankless heater, look closely at the flow rate at the given temperature rise; this tells you how much hot water it can deliver at a constant rate.

GO WITH THE LOW-FLOW

Installing low-flow showerheads and faucet aerators is the easiest way to save energy with hot water. Today's showerheads range from 1 gallon per minute (gpm) flow to 2.5 gpm (compared with 5 gpm of many pre-1992 heads). Aerators can reduce water use to as little as 0.5 gpm.

Indirect

Indirect water heaters are an energy-efficient option for homes with boiler-based space heating systems (although some can be used with furnaces). The water is heated by the boiler and is stored in an insulated tank. When used with a high-efficiency boiler, an indirect system can be the cheapest way to heat water.

Solar for Hot Water

Solar hot water systems have been around since the early 1900s, and they are now beginning to play key roles in the future of sustainable energy use. A typical residential system includes rooftop solar collectors that heat water or an antifreeze solution in a network of tubing. The tubing provides heat energy or usable hot water to a tank or other type of water heater inside the house. Most systems include a conventional heat source in the home to boost the water temperature as needed. There are many types of solar systems and configurations available. To find out what's best for your home and climate, talk to local solar professionals and some competent plumbers who work with solar systems.

Because of its compact size and the fact that it is wall-mounted, a tankless water heater, such as the Rinnai R75LSi, takes up substantially less space than a conventional one.

Adding Insulation

Adding insulation to the attic is relatively easy and is one of the most cost-effective ways to create a comfortable home year-round.

A LOOK AT GREEN INSULATION

The green building movement is changing the way we look at insulation. Any well-built, energy-efficient home needs highly effective insulation, but a green home also strives for safe, sustainably produced products. Here are some insulation products popular with green builders and available for DIY installation.

Cellulose

Available in loose-fill and damp-spray formulations, cellulose insulation is made primarily from recycled newsprint treated with borate for fire-resistance (avoid products treated with ammonium sulfate). Its combination of performance, low-toxicity, and low-impact production makes it one of the greenest options available. Loose-fill versions are suitable for "blowing-in" to an attic to boost insulation levels.

Cotton

Cotton insulation, made without chemical irritants, consists mostly of recycled denim and is completely recyclable. Available in standard sizes of batts, cotton insulation installs much like conventional fiberglass insulation.

Mineral Wool

Mineral wool comes in two types: rock wool (made from natural rock) and slag wool (made from blast-furnace slag, a by-product of steel production). Both offer similar properties, including high fire-resistance, good soundproofing, and relatively high R-values. Slag wool can be made with up to 100-percent recycled content. Mineral wool comes in several forms, including loose-fill and batts, but its availability is limited in many areas.

Fiberglass

Many manufacturers offer greener fiberglass insulation products, in loose-fill, blanket, and batt versions. For healthier and more sustainable products, look for high recycled content (35 percent or more) and products made without formaldehyde. Greenguard certification indicates low chemical emissions.

Rigid-foam Board

Rigid-foam board is useful for sealing large air leaks and other applications where batt insulation is inappropriate. For greener options, look for products made without ozone-depleting blowing agents. Some products are also made with recovered materials.

Natural Wool

Although it's hard to find, wool insulation is very green—sustainable, effective, and irritant-free. It also works well when it gets wet and is completely biodegradable. Wool is available in batt, loose-fill, and rope (for log homes) versions.

Windows

Place larger, insulated windows on the south side of your house with a nearby heat-absorbing wall. This passive solar design significantly reduces your heating needs. Be sure that your replacement windows are Energy Star–rated for your area of the country.

THANKS TO TECHNOLOGICAL ADVANCEMENTS and a shift in design preferences, homes have more windows now than ever before. From an energy perspective, windows offer three main benefits: they bring light into the home and reduce the need for artificial lighting; they help capture free and healthy solar heat; and they provide air-flow for natural ventilation and cooling. If you're thinking about adding new windows, it's important to consider all three of these benefits, which can affect your decisions on the placement, size, type, and energy performance of the new windows.

PLANNING FOR PASSIVE SOLAR AND DAYLIGHTING

Heating your home through strategic window placement is the basic principle behind passive solar design. Daylighting is designers' jargon for using windows to bring in natural light. Both strategies are perfectly simple in theory, yet require careful planning to be most effective for each part of your house.

Planning for passive solar starts with an understanding of the house's orientation to the sun's path throughout the seasons. In general, windows in south-facing walls are best for solar heating, because they get the most direct exposure in winter when the sun is lower in the sky. In summer, when the sun passes more or less overhead, south-facing windows can be easily shaded from direct sunlight by roof overhangs or window awnings, thus minimizing solar heat gain when it's least desirable. Windows on east- and west-facing walls get a lot of direct sunlight in the morning and afternoon, respectively, every season of the year.

Daylighting follows the same principles as passive solar design, but it also takes into account the quality and quantity of available sunlight for each room. For example, rooms with east-facing windows are brightest in the morning, while rooms with west-facing windows are brightest from mid-afternoon until sunset. Placing windows higher on a wall brings light farther into a room's interior. And open floor plans allow multiple spaces to share the same light throughout the day.

WINDOW SHOPPING

These days, windows are available with several high-tech features for fine-tuning performance to meet specific needs throughout the house. Here are some of the key terms and features to look for:

NFRC LABELS

The National Fenestration Rating Council provides official performance ratings for most types of new windows. Look to the NFRC label to compare products for:

• U-factor
• Solar heat gain coefficient (SHGC)
• Visible light transmittance
• Air leakage
• Condensation resistance

Low-e: Low-emissivity coatings are transparent metal films that let light and heat through window glazing but keep heat from escaping. They can also be used to keep heat from coming in (for hot climates).

Gas fill: All energy-efficient windows have two or more panes of glass for insulation. Between the panes, better windows include an inert gas, such as argon or krypton, to minimize heat transfer through the glazing.

Edge spacers: The insulation stripping between panes is critical to window performance and longevity. Better spacers come with long guarantees against failure and offer greater thermal resistance.

Replacing single-pane windows with Energy Star–qualified double-paned ones eliminates the need for cumbersome storm windows.

U-factor: Tells you how well insulated a window is, or how well it isolates indoor and outdoor temperatures. The lower the U-factor, the better.

Solar heat gain coefficient (SHGC): Indicates how much heat is allowed in through the window. The higher the number, the more heat comes through.

Visible light transmittance: Indicates how much light gets through. A lower number means your view of the outdoors is darker. This also considers how much framing a window has.

Air leakage: The measure of airtightness. Windows can leak air at frame joints, glazing seals, and weather seals around each moveable sash.

Condensation resistance: How well the window resists condensation on the inside of the glass. A higher number is better.

MAKE SURE NEW WINDOWS ARE WORTH IT

If you're thinking about replacing your old windows to save energy, it's a good idea to have an energy audit done before making a big investment in new windows. An audit can tell you how much you can expect to save with new windows and can identify other, less-expensive, improvements that may yield comparable savings. You also might consider energy-efficient "replacement" windows—custom-sized inserts that fit into your existing window frames. With proper installation, replacement inserts can offer comparable performance to all-new windows with less expense and remodeling work than complete, or "prime," window replacement.

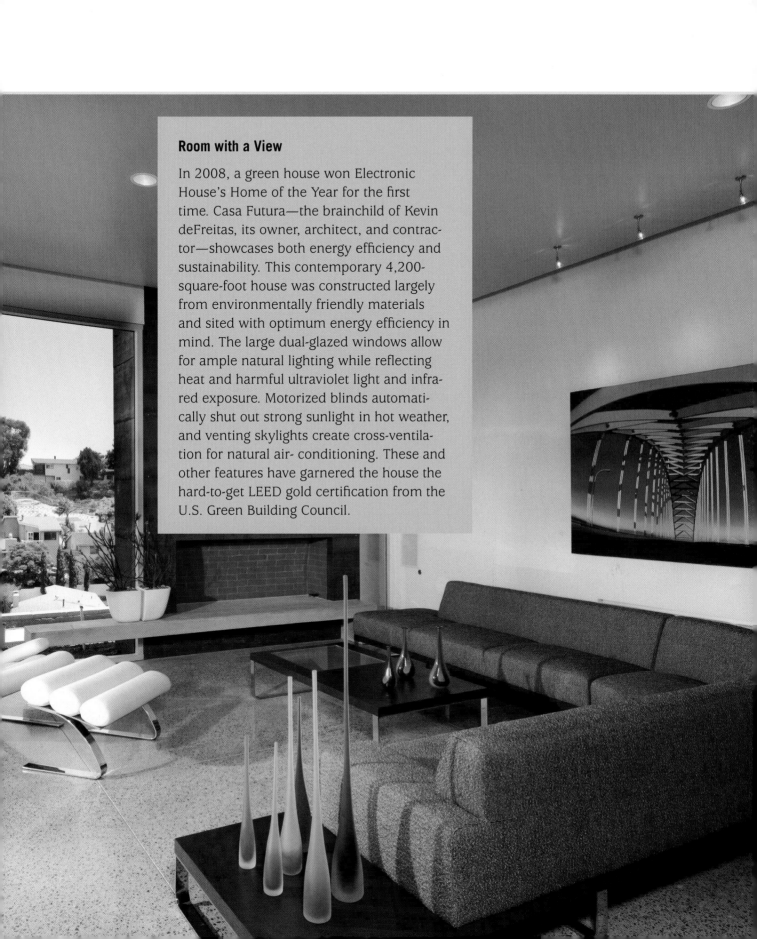

Room with a View

In 2008, a green house won Electronic House's Home of the Year for the first time. Casa Futura—the brainchild of Kevin deFreitas, its owner, architect, and contractor—showcases both energy efficiency and sustainability. This contemporary 4,200-square-foot house was constructed largely from environmentally friendly materials and sited with optimum energy efficiency in mind. The large dual-glazed windows allow for ample natural lighting while reflecting heat and harmful ultraviolet light and infrared exposure. Motorized blinds automatically shut out strong sunlight in hot weather, and venting skylights create cross-ventilation for natural air- conditioning. These and other features have garnered the house the hard-to-get LEED gold certification from the U.S. Green Building Council.

Chapter 4

THE GREEN LIFESTYLE

Living la Vida Verde

MAINTAINING A GREEN LIFESTYLE is just as important as creating a green home. This can include paying attention to how you entertain or celebrate special events, what sort of gifts you give for birthdays or holidays, how you pamper your body, what sort of vacations you take, and how you apply green principles to caring for an infant or child. Even if you are a renter who doesn't own a home, your apartment lifestyle can still reflect a green attitude. Perhaps the most important part of living a green lifestyle is sharing it with your children—by setting a good example and making them part of the process. By educating the next generation, you can be hopeful that they will become smarter, more mindful consumers who will follow in your earth-friendly footsteps.

Green Entertaining

monogrammed linen napkins. And make sure that your candles are made from beeswax or soy, with lead-free wicks.

- If you intend to hire a caterer, bring your own serving dishes and platters to them beforehand; that way you avoid using their disposable trays. Also ask the caterer to use wax paper (biodegradable) or aluminum foil (recyclable) to seal the food instead of plastic wrap.

- If you plan to invest in this and future green get-togethers, shop online for recycled glass bowls or vases, placemats made from recycled chopsticks, and renewable hemp dinner napkins.

WHETHER YOU'RE PLANNING an indoor get-together or a patio barbecue, there are many ways to make the event enjoyable without sacrificing your commitment to conserving energy and reducing carbon emissions.

HOUSE PARTIES

When you're hosting a dinner party, wine-and-cheese gathering, or birthday bash, make sure to use vintage, sustainable or reusable, or recycled materials to decorate your table and organic, locally grown produce on your menu.

- A formal dinner party is the perfect time to unpack your grandmother's lace tablecloth or your mother's

Tips for Green Gatherings

- Decorate your table with natural items you already have around the house—potted plants, a collection of shells in a basket, even a few small botanical prints on easels can add lots of earth-friendly charm.

- When choosing your menu, shop for locally grown produce—whether it's corn for roasting in its husk at a cookout or fresh berries for dessert at your formal dinner. If you're serving chicken, beef, or pork, look for meat that is antibiotic- and hormone-free.

- Make sure that there's a bin located near the trash for recycling, and make its intention clear.

- Send out digital invitations; many invitation Web sites include an online RSVP.

- Ask guests to carpool, if possible.

- When buying beverages for your wine-and-cheese party, opt for glass bottles and aluminum cans, which have a longer recycling life than plastic containers.
- Shop for cheese processed at a local farm, or stick to American-made varieties to avoid the carbon footprint of imports.
- At birthday time, forget the crepe-paper decorations; hang popcorn strings (that later go outside to feed wildlife) or make paper chains from used paper or old magazines instead. If you need balloons for a children's party, look for ones made of recycled latex.

BARBECUES

Even though barbecues take place outdoors and are therefore inherently green—you're not using household lighting, electric appliances, or air conditioning—there are several areas where cookouts do impact the environment.

- Paper plates and plastic cups and utensils may be handy, but they end up in landfills. It's a lot more earth friendly to keep a stock of inexpensive china and cutlery on hand to use for cook-

Add elegance to even the most casual outdoor dining experience with real china, instead of plastic, and a fabric tablecloth.

outs. Or look for durable "paperlike" plates and bowls made from renewable and biodegradable sugar cane.

- If mosquitoes or gnats are a problem, use insect repellents that do not contain harmful DEET to keep those flying pests away.
- Most manufactured charcoal briquettes sold in the United States give off more than 100 times the amount of carbon dioxide—as well as multiple VOCs—than low-emission propane grills. If you just love that smoky flavor, however, consider using real charcoal that is harvested from trees without destroying them, using a method called "coppicing." You can order bags of all-natural charcoal online from Nature's Grilling Products, Cowboy Charcoal, or Wicked Good Charcoal, which comes from Forest Stewardship Council–certified woods. Avoid using lighter fluid; prime your charcoal with small bundles of dry kindling—or order wood wool online.

Don't spoil your all-natural charcoal with lighter fluid; use a crumpled piece of newspaper at the bottom of your charcoal pile or an electric starter for ignition.

Green Weddings and Other Special Occasions

ON YOUR WEDDING DAY, you and your partner will share your commitment to each other with friends and family. Imagine if you could also use this special occasion to share your commitment to living green. Having an earth-friendly wedding isn't difficult, and with a little creativity, you can make it an event that stands out in everyone's mind for its originality and eco-friendly spirit.

The following tips and suggestions will help you lower the overall carbon footprint of your engagement and wedding.

Wedding and engagement rings: Gold mining typically results in vast amounts of pollution—producing one gold ring creates 20 tons of mine waste—so look for vintage rings or ones crafted from recycled precious metal. Alternatively, repurpose a piece of heirloom jewelry into a ring. Diamonds may be a girl's best friend, but these days there is a risk that they could be smuggled "conflict" or "blood" diamonds used to fund rebel forces in Africa. Consider sapphires, rubies, emeralds, and other precious gems instead.

Wedding registry: Add TerraPass.com to your registry to receive special wedding gift carbon offsets for travel. If you are requesting appliances as gifts, make sure you specify Energy Star.

Invitations: Many wedding invitation retailers now offer recycled or partially recycled paper stock for invitations, response cards, and envelopes. The more ambitious could also consider making your own paper from shredded waste paper and cloth. Add lavender or other dried flowers to the mix for a unique and beautiful texture. Ask an artistic friend to hand letter the invitations with soy-based ink. Check out the many online sites that offer instructions for handmade paper. Although it's quite nontraditional, the greenest choice of all is to send paper-free online invitations. Evite.com offers a wide range of wedding and bridal shower invitations and also features links to gift registries.

Your recycled gold bands might be derived from an old PC, scrap gold, or out-of-style jewelry; both high-end and more affordable consumer outlets have taken the "no dirty gold" pledge.

Flowers needn't be exotic to be lovely. Choose local species rather than imports for a freshly elegant eco-friendly bouquet.

Bridal bouquets: Many flowers are imported from countries that still use harmful pesticides, so look for a florist shop that uses organic, locally grown flowers in its arrangements.

Wedding entertainment: Rather than driving all over to see potential wedding bands play, ask them to send you DVDs of weddings at which they have performed. Or consider using a DJ—one person in one car, rather than several band members driving from different cities.

Table favors: Your guests will be charmed if you offer them something more sustainable than the usual embossed pen or engraved wine glass as a table favor. Fill a gauzy bag with a variety of colorful seed packets, or offer fair-trade chocolate-covered espresso beans or locally made chocolates wrapped with a bright ribbon.

Food and drink: Look for caterers who use organic food and/or local produce. Make sure that they offer at least one vegetarian option. Patronize a local winery or brewery when ordering alcoholic beverages for your reception.

Centerpieces: Decorate each table with bamboo in a watery vase or a flowering garden plant in a pretty pot. You can also use dried flowers from your garden to create centerpieces as well as floral swags to decorate the walls and serving tables.

Honeymoon: Check out the eco-friendly resorts listed at Green Globe 21 (www.greenglobe21.com); the Greener Lodging Directory (www.greenerlodging.com); Great Green Travel (greatgreentravel.com); International Ecotourism Society (www.ecotourism.org); and Organic Travel (www.organic-travel.com).

Many of these ideas for green invitations, decorations, and catering can also be used for bar/bat mitzvahs, anniversaries, graduations, birthdays, and other family celebrations.

Decorate reception tables with bamboo shoots that guests can take home and repot. Live plants make great mementos of your special day.

Green Celebration Basics

- Use recycled paper or send online invitations.
- Rent all supplies, such as linens, tents, place settings, tables, and chairs.
- Register for or purchase carbon offsets to mitigate any celebration-related travel by car or air.
- Opt for locally grown organic produce and organic meat.

Green Giving

SHOW YOUR FRIENDS YOU CARE about them and the earth by giving eco-friendly presents. Need something for a housewarming, wedding, birthday, or anniversary? Your options have just gotten greener.

GREEN THE HOMES OF FRIENDS AND FAMILY

Green as can be, plants are wonderful gifts. Potted indoor plants liven up rooms and clean your air. A whole range of flowers from orchids to African violets will bloom cyclically—an event to look forward to and a reminder of you. Aloes are handy for cooks who inevitably come away from a brilliant meal with a burn. Giving to a loved one with a brown thumb? Consider a cactus.

Herbs are wonderfully fragrant and edible gifts. For city dwellers, buy a rectangular box or herbarium, extra soil, and some seeds or starter plants bought from the local farmer's market. Easy-care herbs include rosemary, sage, thyme, and parsley. Once established, herbs like chives, mint, and tarragon will survive the winter and can be kept outside.

FROM TREES TO TECHNOLOGY

Plant a tree to commemorate a wedding or birthday. It's a gift with a truly positive environmental impact—and you'll enjoy seeing your gift grow and prosper over the years.

Think about the backyard. Nature enthusiasts will appreciate a birdhouse or feeder. Research species indigenous to the area and purchase an appropriate home, plus a field guide and/or binoculars so friends know what they're looking at. Help outfit a deck with wicker chairs or other furniture made from renewable materials.

Use your purchasing power to encourage

> "The only gift is a portion of thyself."
>
> —Ralph Waldo Emerson

Planet-friendly Gifts

Green gifts are available for everybody. Approach gift buying with an eye toward the environment, and you will quickly see hundreds of options. Here are just a few choices:

- Fair-trade chocolates, coffee, tea, and other products that are grown and harvested—and the income distributed—in a socially and environmentally conscious manner.

- Products ranging from cutting boards to skateboards made from renewable bamboo.

- Create your own gift basket of locally made goodies from the farmer's market. Bring a biodynamic wine or locally brewed beer to a holiday party or barbecue. Have a garden? Bring home-dried herbs or tomato sauce you canned yourself.

- Homemade gifts, such as baked goods or infused olive oil made with garden herbs.

- Energy-saving devices, such as solar chargers for computers or other electronics.

fun outdoor activities with bicycles and bike helmets, in-line skates, a pet from the local animal shelter, or green camping goods such as solar cookers and solar-powered tents.

For domestic bliss, give a luxurious set of organic linens or pillows made from natural fibers. For health at the studio, give a yoga mat made of earth-friendly materials. For fun, give a colorful welcome mat constructed from old flip-flops. Your foodie friend will surely appreciate a set of graceful cooking utensils or downy-soft dish towels made of renewable bamboo. Chefs always appreciate a good cookbook; explore those with exciting vegetarian options or a focus on seasonal ingredients.

Techies will be surprised to learn that not all gadgets are made of nonbiodegradable plastic. In stores are items such as iPod cases processed from recycled materials, and monitors and mice made from the incredibly versatile bamboo.

NO WRAPPING REQUIRED

Sometimes the best gifts are those that occupy no space at all. Or perhaps they are as small as a membership card or gift certificate. Know a couple that hates to clean? For their anniversary give a gift certificate for an eco-friendly cleaning service. Offer your own services. Babysit for a night and give tired parents a rest and a night out. Give outdoorsy folks passes to a national park or local preserve or memberships to the Sierra or Appalachian Mountain clubs. Give art and music lovers a membership to a museum or tickets to a concert. For mediaphiles, provide an online subscription to a favorite newspaper or magazine. Have a friend who likes to get around? Give a gift membership for a Zipcar or other car-rental service.

Gift certificates to local restaurants are a great way to fete your family and support community businesses. Also on the edible end, give a share to a Community Supported Agriculture farm—fresh produce as long as the growing season lasts!

The Gift of Time

Do something together. Rock out at a benefit concert; take knitting lessons (using locally made wool); attend a tasting of biodynamic or organic wines. Take your friend on a hike, and bring a picnic. Volunteer together.

Offer to offset the carbon footprint of a honeymoon. Carbon offset organizations contribute to the research and development of renewable energy sources, plant trees, and help out communities and local economies negatively impacted by tourism.

Maybe what you'd most like to do is give your friend or family member a little climate change education. This doesn't have to be a drag—far from it. A few fun and social options include the award-winning film *An Inconvenient Truth*; National Parks Monopoly, which features parks from Acadia to Yellowstone; and fascinating books on where your food comes from or green building.

Donations are heartfelt and often overlooked gifts. Find out what organizations are close to the heart, and give in your friends' and family's name. To celebrate anniversaries and big birthdays, host a fund-raising party and give the proceeds to the honoree's favorite charity. For the holidays, make a family decision not to give gifts but to pool your money and donate to an agreed-upon organization. Nonpolluting and guilt-free, what could be a better gift than bettering the world together?

An Eco-friendly Holiday

HAVING AN ECO-FRIENDLY HOLIDAY does not mean that it has to be any less festive. It just requires a little extra thought. For instance, what is better: a live Christmas tree or an artificial one? Which holiday lights use the least amount of energy? How do I decorate with the environment in mind? What makes a good, but planet-friendly gift, and what is the best way to wrap it?

LIVE VERSUS ARTIFICIAL

Which is better for the environment: artificial trees that last for many years but are made of plastic, or live Christmas trees that are natural products, but only last a few weeks?

Some people favor artificial trees, citing that they are reusable and therefore more ecologically sound than cutting down a live tree every year. Yet, detractors point out that most artificial trees are made of polyvinyl chloride (or PVC) plastic. Derived from petroleum, PVC is made by a process that produces various potential pollutants, including the carcinogen vinyl chloride monomer. Detractors also note that most families toss out their trees in 5 to 10 years. It then gets dumped into a landfill where it may remain for centuries.

THE REAL THING

Live trees have short shelf lives, their needles fall off, sap can drip onto the floor, and dried-out ones can be fire hazards. Nonetheless, proponents assert that live trees are the most planet-friendly choice. The trees, which may need 6, 8, or even 15 years or more to reach holiday size, are cleaning the atmosphere the entire time they are growing. An acre of Christmas trees can absorb thousands of pounds of carbon dioxide, while producing enough oxygen for as many as 18 people. According to the environmental restoration group American Forests, the annual U.S. crop of Christmas trees produces enough oxygen to meet the needs of 18 million people.

Another option is a live, rooted tree. It requires some extra effort, including a gradual introduction from outdoors to indoors and vice versa.

GREEN DECORATIONS

LED lights: One of the simplest ways to save energy during the holidays is to switch from strings of the typical incandescent lights to strings of LED lights. LED (light-emitting diode) lights give the same effect as conventional bulbs, but use only 10 to 20 percent of the energy. They last longer, too. Add a timer to automatically turn them off, and you can save even more on energy.

▲ Beeswax candles add a festive glow and a honey scent.

▶ String popcorn and cranberries for a biodegradable holiday garland that evokes times past while protecting the future.

Wreaths and garlands: Live wreaths and garlands make sense for the same reasons that live trees do. Sometimes, tree sellers offer free branches that they have trimmed off their cut trees. With the help of a reusable wire wreath frame available at any craft store, you can create a fresh and aromatic wreath. Add flowers, pinecones, and fresh fruit to design a wreath to match your decor. Gardeners may also consider building a wreath partially or fully from fresh or dried herbs grown in the yard. Often, you can remove these herbs after the holiday season and use them for cooking.

Festive lighting: Candles are popular holiday decorations, and natural beeswax candles are eco-friendly options. Beeswax not only has a pleasant honey and flower-nectar scent, but it is also a naturally renewable resource and burns both cleaner and longer than the traditionally used paraffin.

WRAP IT UP!

The finishing touch is green packaging. For children, gifts wrapped in comic pages from old newspapers are perfect. For other packages, consider wrapping them in old maps or posters. Another good option is a colorful shopping bag or a reusable, fabric gift bag. Saved ribbons and bows can be used again and again. You can also make your own toppers out of collected pinecones.

When mailing gifts, avoid non-biodegradable foam packaging peanuts. Alternatives include wadded old newspaper, starch-based peanuts that dissolve in water and are safe for the environment, and biodegradable peanuts made from recycled paper products.

Earth-friendly Products for Babies and Children

BABY ESSENTIALS AND CLOTHING

Diapers are perennially ecologically tricky, but generally speaking, there are better alternatives to standard disposables. A few companies now make biodegradable diapers, along with flushable diapers and baby wipes. Many parents have found cotton diapers to be easy to use and clean. They're also significantly cheaper. Disposable diapers often occupy a shockingly high percentage of the baby-care budget.

Just as companies are manufacturing organic cotton or hemp wardrobes for adults, they're also selling a variety of soft and cute baby clothes. Consumers now have a choice among many lines of earth-friendly goods—from hats to shoes—made of organic materials.

YOUR CHILDREN MAY ACT WISE beyond their years, but their bodies are delicate and need to be protected. From bathing to playing, there are a number of ways to green up the lives of little ones.

BATHING

There's no getting around it—kids get dirty. When handing over that bar of soap or plopping your child in the tub, think about the products you're using. Are the cleansers gentle and nontoxic? Read the labels. Go for fragrance-free, or soap with only plant-based oils, such as lavender and lemon verbena. Use a naturally soft sea sponge; they resist bacteria and mold more easily than synthetic ones. Dry your babies down with organic cotton towels and wrap them in bamboo fabric robes.

Buy brushes (tooth and hair) made from wood, bamboo, and hygienic animal hair.

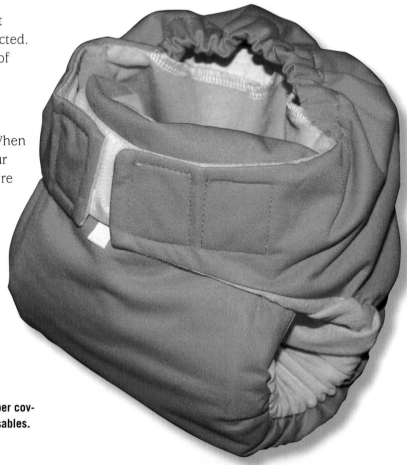

A fitted organic cotton diaper fits neatly inside a wool diaper cover and makes babies less prone to diaper rash than disposables.

Eco-friendly pacifiers use natural rubber instead of chemically tainted silicone.

Baby food has also gone organic, with a wide variety of flavors from a growing number of manufacturers, including the major baby food companies, such as Gerber and Beechnut.

GEAR

Comfort infants with an all-natural rubber pacifier. Feed them with glass bottles or plastic ones free of dangerous bisphenol A. Shop for organic play mats, changing table covers, carriers, and to lug everything around, several tote bags. When the day is done, put your baby to bed between organic sheets fitted on an all-natural bed. You'll sleep better, too.

Unpainted and uncoated blocks are best for a baby, who can enjoy these playthings for many years as a toddler, preschooler, or even grade schooler.

TOYS

All sizes of kids can now toss around a host of toys made of organic cotton and lamb's wool. Look for playthings made of uncoated and unstained wood. Blocks, puzzles, and other building tools are perfect examples. Keep an eye out for Fair Trade labels on imported goods. Send your kid to class with a backpack constructed from recycled plastic bottles; inside pack a lunch in a reusable cotton or thermal bag, and include an old-school jump rope with wooden handles and organic cotton rope.

Think Old-fashioned

Many everyday items are transformed into great toys by sheer imagination. Try giving your baby a pair of wooden spoons. Help an older child make a rag doll with scraps of material and rubber bands. Some of the best games are invented with toys picked up around the house.

The Green Goddess: Body Products and Skin Care

Natural loofah soap combines the moisturizing effects of glycerine with the exfoliating properties of a loofah.

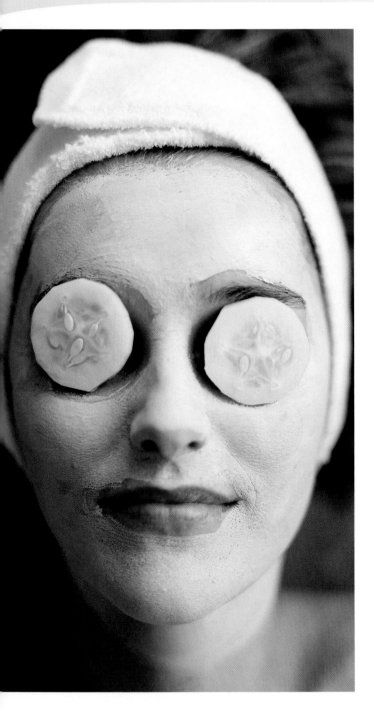

Stock your shower or bath with some of these body-care items:

- All-natural loofah and sea sponges
- Stone made of real pumice
- Wooden and natural fiber nailbrush
- Organic cotton and hemp shower curtain
- Organic soaps and cleansers scented with plant oils
- Recycled and recyclable razor

Step out of the bath and towel down with soft organic cotton or bamboo towels. Use biodegradable makeup cloths and tissues. Layer on a "nut butter" moisturizer made without petroleum jelly. Support small businesses and farms by purchasing locally made products

The ingredients in this all-natural mascara include organic beeswax, aloe vera, grapefruit seed extract, and mica.

EARTH-FRIENDLY BATHING AND BEAUTY products are an expanding market. From cleansers to cotton balls to concealer, any woman can become a green goddess.

whenever possible. Look for the USDA certified organic seal. Be wary of labels that contain a long list of items that you don't recognize and sound like synthetics. Know that "hydrosol" is a fancy name for a water-based product that likely contains chemical substances. Look up products in the Skin Deep database, created by the Environmental Working Group. The database provides a safety rating based on the product's components.

Give yourself a manicure using polish free of phthalates and polish remover without acetone or acetate. Avoid any nail salons that knock you over with noxious fumes when you open the door.

If you like a little color on your face, there are plenty of earth- and body-friendly makeup lines. Remember that ancient societies used henna, berries, and natural dyes—the original earth tones. In "civilized" Europe, a pale white face was preferred, leading women to apply lead paint to their faces. Thankfully the pendulum is swinging back to non-poisonous ingredients, such as beeswax, plant oils, and even mica—yes, the sparkly stuff that flakes off rocks. Many responsible, environmentally conscious companies are now offering nontoxic and beautiful products. Go ahead and treat yourself—just read the labels.

Organic soaps, bath salts, and candles—bought at your local farmer's market—can take a restorative bath to the next level.

Let the Buyer Beware

Stay away from these top toxins.

- Phthalates (found in nail polish, and some hair sprays, cosmetics, and perfumes)
- Lead (in some hair coloring and lipstick)
- Petroleum products (found in hair coloring, nail polish, shampoo, and most toothpastes, petroleum-based products have many names, most of them long and unpronounceable)
- Mercury (also called thimerosal)
- Fragrance (an entirely unregulated catchall term)
- Formaldehyde (a preservative also known as formalin, formic aldehyde, and oxymethylene)
- Propylene glycol (found in many moisturizers)
- PABA (in some sunscreens and lip balm)

Apartment Living: Going Green in Smaller Spaces

GREEN LIVING ISN'T RESTRICTED TO OWNERS of detached houses. Apartment dwellers have plenty of opportunities to be earth friendly, too. In fact, people who live in apartments are already fairly green, because apartment buildings make more efficient use of their physical footprint than single-family dwellings. They are also frequently close to mass transit, shopping, and restaurants, eliminating the need for a car.

There is a downside, however. Apartment residents suffer much poorer air quality than homeowners, the result of limited ventilation, combined with exposure to gas stoves, cigarette smoke, and emissions from manufacturing chemicals, such as the formaldehyde in composite wood.

Nevertheless, there are many things you can do as a renter to improve your quality of life and reduce your carbon footprint. A first step is getting on good terms with your landlord or management office. You'll need permission to start a recycling center in your basement, for instance (though in many locales, this is mandated by law), or to request low-VOC (volatile organic compound) paints when your unit is due for repainting. You might also want to discuss some eco-friendly, money-saving options with your landlord, such as using fluorescent light bulbs in the hallways, and switching to Energy Star appliances or installing double-paned windows in the units. For the most part, though, you'll be on your own when it comes to creating a green living space. And even though you're only a renter, you can still make significant improvements.

Moving Green

- Have an apartment sale to get rid of stuff you no longer want.
- If you need to purchase new moving boxes, get ones made with a high percentage of recycled paper.
- Pack suitcases and duffels—you'll be moving them anyway.
- Rent hanging clothing boxes.
- Use old newspapers for packing.

The New Apartment

If you're apartment hunting, here's a list of things to look for before you make the decision to sign the lease.

- Check a potential apartment for heat, air, and moisture leakage, especially around windows and doors.
- Ask the real estate agent about recycling, garbage, and composting policies.
- Ask about connections to mass transit.
- Check to see if the appliances are energy-efficient.

TIPS FOR A GREENER APARTMENT

- Caulk any leaky windows, and place door stripping along the bottom sills. Also seal around the air conditioner.

- Replace ceiling lights with compact fluorescent light bulbs. They last 10 times longer than regular bulbs and use one third the power.

- Install a low-flow showerhead—and save nearly 4,000 gallons of water a year. And remember that short showers under 10 minutes long use less water than bathing.

- Put a weighted-down glass jar or plastic bottle in the toilet tank so that it takes less water to refill the tank (don't use bricks, which crumble).

- Put aerators on all your faucets to save water and lower water-heating costs.

- Cook with microwave ovens, toaster ovens, slow cookers, and rice cookers, which concentrate the heat in the food.

- If there's a heater in your unit, change the air filter each fall.

- Fill your apartment with plants—nature's own air purifiers.

- Use greener cleaners or a solution of white vinegar in the kitchen and bath.

- To discourage insects, put a small plate of boric acid near all cabinet openings.

- Install an Energy Star ceiling fan to reduce the use of your air conditioner. Don't forget to use it on reverse in the winter to disperse heat from the ceiling.

- Recycle all paper, glass, plastic, and aluminum. If your building doesn't provide recycling options, ask your landlord about starting one.

- If you have a dog, take biodegradable pooper-scoop bags with you on walks.

- Give your pets a little "patch of green" to nibble on by planting grass seed in a pot.

- If you live in an area that gets its electricity from highly polluting coal-fired plants, be extra careful with electrical use, or opt for green energy from your local supplier.

- Don't overlook local resources—from a moving neighbor's apartment sale or discards—to furnish or decorate your space.

- If you're a diehard green advocate, you can compost on your deck or patio. The Envirocycle Spinning Composter and the NatureMill automatic composter are two models made for apartment dwellers.

- Try a green dry cleaner.

- Visit the local farmer's market.

Going Green on Vacation

GO NONSTOP

Airplanes use the most fuel per minute during takeoff and landing, so if you avoid the added time and inconvenience of hopping from one plane to the next, you'll get where you want to go sooner and lower your carbon footprint.

WE ALL LIVE FOR VACATION: time away from work and responsibilities; time to spend with loved ones or exploring a new environment. The planet, though, can be an unintended casualty of our pleasure if we're not careful. Next time you go away, think about these green strategies for reducing the impact of your vacation on the earth.

MAKING THE SKIES FRIENDLIER

You're going away, but how will you get there? Airplanes, most of which were built during decades of cheap oil, are fossil-fuel fiends. They are, however, the fastest, easiest, and sometimes only way to reach your destination. And you can offset the carbon footprint of your flights.

Offsets are usually measured in tons, with one offset equal to the reduction of one metric ton of carbon dioxide, or its equivalent in other green-

Book flights with airlines that offer electronic tickets to reduce paper waste. You'll also avoid long lines at the ticket counter.

house gases. Offset projects achieve this by supporting renewable energy, such as wind, solar, and biofuels, improving the energy efficiency of industry, capturing emissions, and planting trees. Your contribution will often be tax deductible. Do a little research before writing your check, though. Make sure your money is going where you want it to go.

Wherever the destination, check out the local public transportation. In many countries, the airports are connected to cities by cheap and efficient trains, trams, or buses. To get around once you're there, walk to absorb local life, or rent bikes or mopeds to cover more ground. If you need to rent a car, check if your company has hybrids in its fleet, or buy a carbon offset.

LOOKING FOR GREEN ACCOMMODATIONS

As ecotourism and earth-friendly travel become more important to consumers, companies are adjusting to their demands. There are many ways for hotels and other lodgings to be green. They may use renewable energy sources, reduce consumption and waste, use green cleaning products,

Choose a resort that makes a low impact on the environment and the local culture, while contributing to local employment and ecosystem conservation.

or give back to their local communities through donations or charity work.

Consider where and how the hotel is built. Were fragile forests, beaches, or wetlands destroyed or disturbed to build your lodge? How have hotel practices affected the local community?

While staying, pretend that you're paying the energy bill. This means remembering to turn off lights and TV when you leave the room, not letting hot shower water run while you're not in it, and reusing towels and sheets for a few days before handing them over to housekeeping.

Carbon offsets help to finance this reforestation project in Burkina Faso, which prevents the spread of desertification.

CERTIFIED CARBON OFFSETS

You can purchase carbon offsets to counteract your emissions, but what really happens to your money when you buy them? Many organizations can prove that they're doing what they're supposed to with third-party certification standards, verification, and auditing. Advocates disagree on what method of certification is best. Some of the most respected names in certification are Green-e Energy, Environmental Resources Trust (ERT), The Climate, Community & Biodiversity Standards (CCBS), Voluntary Carbon Standard (VCS), and The Gold Standard.

Chapter 5

MAKE YOUR CLEANING GREEN

Low-impact Cleaning Products

YOUR HOME IS YOUR REFUGE from the outside world. It should be a safe, clean place.

Yet the use of home decorating and cleaning products can render indoor air even more toxic than outdoor air. You can green up your cleaning act by using truly natural and biodegradable cleaning products—you'll be surprised at the superior results. Reduce the energy drained by everyday household appliances. Evaluate the life you share with your pets: is their care as green as can be? Finally, take a look at household waste. A few simple guidelines will help lighten your trash load and be more friendly to the planet.

Getting Clean with Less Effort and Energy

WE ALL LIKE A CLEAN HOME, but not if it comes at the expense of health.

If you want your home to smell like the beautiful outdoors, open a window or set out a vase of fresh flowers. Discard air fresheners and use low-impact naturally fragranced cleaners. The chemicals in these are released into the air we breathe.

Consider your alternatives carefully by reading labels. Don't be fooled by slogans like "all-natural" and "eco-friendly." These designations are not government regulated, so a manufacturer has no obligation to back up this claim. Ingredients should include plant-based elements, such as grain alcohol and nut and herb oils, instead of unpronounceable synthetics. Avoid chlorine and ammonia, both hazardous to your health. (Never ever combine the two: they create cholramine, a toxic gas.)

Organic foods can be a bit more costly, but the same doesn't have to be true of organic cleaning products, because you probably already have much of what you need right in your pantry. Inexpensive household ingredients, such as baking soda, white vinegar, and castile soap, plus water, can be transformed into really effective cleaners. Baking soda, an excellent abrasive, combats fungus hiding in sinks and tubs and on tile. Vinegar

MAKE YOUR OWN CLEANSER

Here's a simple green recipe to replace a common toxic cleaner:

Homemade Liquid Scouring Cleanser

Ingredients:

½ cup baking soda

2–4 squirts green liquid soap or detergent (good brands include Ecover's all-purpose soap and Dr. Bronner's castile soap)

1. Put baking soda in a bowl.
2. Stir in enough soap or detergent to make a frosting-like texture.
3. Scoop onto a sponge and scrub away.

sanitizes by erasing bacteria. Spray or sponge it onto nonmarble countertops and wood (even wood floors). Add a little lemon juice to the mix for a fresh scent. If soap is needed, the mild castile is cheap and easily available in liquid form.

Remember that your home, contrary to product commercials, is not crawling with deadly organisms. Spend the majority of your labors in the kitchen, where the safe handling of meats and proper disposal of food products will reduce and eliminate bacteria. Change

Acidic lemons kill bacteria and leave a fresh citrus scent. The fruit's natural bleaching properties can also eliminate stains.

Clean Your Fridge, A/C, Furnace, and Chimney to Make Them Run Better

Your refrigerator or freezer is likely the biggest energy-consuming kitchen appliance. A few simple tricks will help it run more efficiently.

- Vacuum the coils. Keep them free of dust and accumulated dirt.
- Clean the gasket and sealing surfaces to ensure that they are airtight.
- Cover liquids and wrap foods to prevent moisture release that makes the compressor work harder.
- Sponge out the trays as needed. The fridge fan will otherwise blow that moldy air right into the kitchen.

Make your air conditioner last longer and work more efficiently through periodic upkeep.

- Clean evaporating and condenser coils.

- Clean or change filters monthly, and clean the cooling coils and fan blades as needed.
- Clean condensate drain, controls, and air filters.

To breathe easier and reduce energy bills, pay attention to your heating system.

- Dust furnaces before they kick on for the winter.
- Clean your oil burner.
- Clean your chimney. This will prevent chimney fires and carbon-monoxide buildup in your home. If you're not running your chimney, seal the damper well. If you never use your chimney, plug and seal it, or pay

dishrags and sponges frequently. Then turn to the vinegar, baking soda, and salt to clean.

Drains can be unclogged in three short steps without the use of toxic commercial preparations and with a little elbow grease.

1. Pour baking soda down the drain.
2. Follow with vinegar.
3. Use what's called a "snake," available at the hardware store. Unwind this plastic tubing–coated wire down the drain until the clog is found, and dredge it up.

If you want to clean green but have big jugs of chemical cleaners left over, don't let them sit around in the garage. Dispose of them properly. This may mean a trip to the household hazardous-waste site. Coordinate with your neighbors to bring all your waste together—and spread the word about the dangers of these cleaners.

The Dollar Bill Test

Do the dollar bill test: If you close the door on a dollar bill and can easily pull it out, replace the gasket.

Laundry, Dishwashing, Bath, and Shower

WATER IS QUICKLY becoming one of the world's most coveted resources. To help out the planet and keep energy dollars in your pocket, use only as much water—especially hot water—as you need. Heating water accounts for between 14 and 25 percent of the energy your home eats up. Attention to every-day activities, such as laundry, dishwashing, and bathing, can really cut back on excess energy use.

If you're in need of a new washer for clothes or dishes, purchase an energy-efficient one. Keep in mind that the Energy Star machines—though more expensive at the store—will save you money in the long run by making your operating costs lower year after year.

If you're sticking with the machines that you have, you can still make a dent in your water and heating bills by cutting down on hot water use.

OTHER THINGS YOU CAN DO

Don't tolerate drips: Fix leaks in fixtures—faucets and showerheads—and pipes. One drip per second from a single leak quickly adds up to a dollar a month.

Aerating showerheads have a lower flow rate than conventional heads, but they provide higher pressure than most water misers.

Front-loading washers use gravity to wash clothing more thoroughly while using less water than top-loading washing machines.

Go with the low flow: Install low-flow fixtures. Investments of just $10 to $20 per fixture can reduce your water use by 25 to 60 percent.

For showerheads, select one with a flow rate of lower than 2.5 gallons per minute (gpm).

Kitchen faucets (known as aerators) should allow 2.2 gpm or fewer, and bathroom faucets from .5 to 1.5 gpm. For maximum efficiency, find an aerator that allows only 1 gpm.

Make a habit of using the short-wash cycle, and turn the water heater down just a notch. You'll save energy and money.

Wash but don't dry: Even if you love handwashing every plate and spoon, consider using the dishwasher. Cleaning a full load of dishes is often more energy efficient.

Short wash cycles also reduce water use. Some dishwashers include a booster heater. This feature is either attached to or inside your washer and heats only the water going straight to the dishes. This machine-specific boost means you can turn the water heater down a notch or two, which will lower the cost of running your dishwasher, as most of the energy used (as much as 80 percent) by your dishwasher is to heat the water.

Organic Beds and Bedding

One place you might not think to green is actually where you spend at least a third of your time: your bed. Increasingly, natural fibers are being used to make both wonderful mattresses and sheets. Your synthetic mattress may be cushy, but it likely emits toxic chemicals. Of great concern is the addition of flame retardants known as PBDEs. These chemicals aren't bound to the mattress material, and so they are able to escape into the air.

The problem with sheets is often the dyes, not to mention the chemical fertilizers heaped on the cotton plants to grow the raw material (about 1.5 pounds per set of sheets). Wrinkle-free sheets stay that way not from fairy dust, but formaldehyde, which can cause skin and eye irritation and, ironically, insomnia.

For a better night's sleep, go natural. Mattresses made with natural fibers are more expensive but last longer than synthetic ones.

A wide range of boutique and commercial companies now offer lines of organic sheets that are both good for the planet and your sleep. Bamboo sheets are naturally microbial. Hemp doesn't have to be the raw scratchy stuff of those brown braided bracelets—it's a fabric now embraced by high-life celebrities. Would Julia Roberts wear a T-shirt that feels like a hair shirt?

Pets

WE ALL RECOGNIZE environmental hazards that people should avoid, but what about your pets? Keep them healthy and their world naturally green through attention to their food, fun, and cleanliness.

The preservatives in commercially grown (read: with lots of chemical fertilizers) wheat and corn in regular dog foods can cause allergy symptoms, such as hair loss and itching. On the protein side, take the meat, skip the hormones. Hormone-injected animal waste harms ecosystems and humans, so how could your pet be immune?

Also consider that the meat in many pet foods is 4-D, the rating that the slaughterhouse gives to animals that are "Dead, Dying, Diseased, or Down." Be wary of the word "by-product" —often code for Don't Eat This. Remember that assurances like "premium" and "gourmet" are not FDA regulated and are no guarantee of high-quality ingredients.

Perhaps the healthiest option for your pup is to make her food yourself. Dogs need a balance of protein, vegetables, and carbohydrates; many simple home recipes are available.

OTHER THINGS YOU CAN DO

Play safe: We love to indulge our pets, but some toys are better left on the shelf. If that stick in the yard leaves your pet cold, know that natural, sustainable fibers such as hemp or butcher bones make great toys. Buy pet beds and accessories made from recycled materials or organic cotton.

Get a checkup: Even if your own last physical was in 1980, take your pets to the veterinarian for their annual vaccines.

Keep them flea- and odor-free: Over-the-counter flea medications are like many name-brand cleaning products: toxic. Use these products only as a last resort. Instead, maintain a naturally clean regimen. If you have indoor pets, vacuum regularly and keep up bathing and brushing routines. If problems persist, use herbal repellants. Adding garlic and brewer's yeast to your pet's food may also keep away pesky fleas.

Stop Overpopulation

To keep the domestic animal kingdom fun, friendly, and in check, consider adopting a dog or cat from a shelter. Nearly every city houses dozens of animals in need of good homes. Once you've decided on a furry mate, prevent unwanted and uncared-for litters by spaying or neutering your pet.

Pet Do's and Don'ts

- Do pick up your dog's poo in a bio-degradable plastic bag. Regular plastic bags seal organic waste that would otherwise decompose.

- Don't leave the mess for someone else to clean up or, worse, wash into a drain and pollute the local water supply.

- Do buy eco- and pet-friendly litters. Safe, biodegradable materials include corn, wheat husks, recycled newspapers, green tea leaves, and recycled pine.

- Don't buy clumping clay cat litter. The clay is strip-mined in planet-unfriendly ways and then some nasty chemicals are added. Carcinogenic silica dust coats your kitty's lungs. The clumping agent sodium benton-ite expands once ingested and can cause harmful digestive blockages.

Skunk Antidotes

If Rover meets a skunk, don't reach for any old shampoo. Visit http://home.earthlink. net/~skunkremedy/home for an antidote. Just as you'd use gentle soaps on your own body, read the labels of pet fur cleansers. Avoid those with toxic chemicals.

Trash and Recycling

IT'S AN OLDIE BUT GOODIE: Reduce, Reuse, Recycle. In that order. The three R's have become a mindset embraced by many—but not enough. Americans still throw too much away. A little effort can go a long way in lightening your trash load and creating a more earth-friendly environmental impact.

LESS IS MORE

Your priority should be throwing less stuff away. That means you should be conscious of what you acquire and in what form it comes. Recycling is appealing and definitely useful, but those recycling plants are powered by fuel.

Before you toss that empty water or beverage bottle, check for its plastics code: if it reads 1 or 2, the bottle is usually recyclable.

At the supermarket, choose the product with less packaging. Pick up loose or unpackaged produce. At the hardware store, see if the items you want (such as nails and screwdrivers) are available individually in bins. As much as possible, buy in bulk.

If you're an online shopper, try to consolidate your orders into fewer packages. Receive as little paper mail as possible. Which bills have online statements? Review your magazine subscriptions and catalogs: which can you view online?

WHAT THE NUMBERS ON THE PLASTIC MEAN

 PETE (polyethylene terephthalate ethylene) used for most sodas, water, juices, detergents, cleansers, and some peanut butter jars.

 HDPE (high density polyethylene) used for milk and water jugs, bleaches, detergents, and some body products.

 PVC or V (polyvinyl chloride) used for cling film, some plastic squeeze bottles, cooking oil, and some detergent and window cleaning preparations.

 LDPE (low density polyethylene) used in most grocery store bags, most plastic wrap, and some bottles.

 PP (polypropylene) used in most opaque/clouded plastic food storage, syrup and yogurt containers, straws, and some baby bottles.

 PS (polystyrene) used in Styrofoam trays and egg cartons, disposable cups and bowls, carryout containers, and opaque plastic cutlery.

 OTHER (usually polycarbonate) used in some baby bottles, water cooler refills, trashcan liners, and some clear plastic cutlery.

Source: Institute for Agriculture and Trade Policy

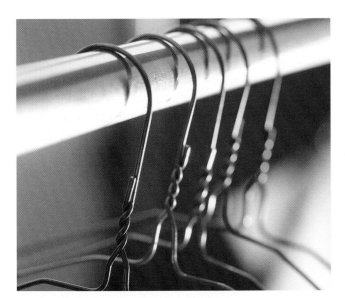

Alleviate closet clutter and make your dry cleaner happy: return those seemingly self-propagating wire hangers.

A SECOND LIFE

Next, take a step back from the trash can. Before your throw out that chair, computer, or set of measuring cups, think: can someone else use this item? Make a quick buck by selling your goods online through Web sites such as Craigslist or eBay. Brainstorm a list of local charities, and keep a list of what they want. The next time you get a new cell phone, give your old one to a veteran's organization or women's shelter. Donate old eyeglasses to a worthy organization, such as Eyes for the Needy.

"Freecycling" has become a popular and fun method of Earth-friendly redistribution. Freecycle, a community-based enterprise, is an online bulletin board organized by geographic area. You post a request for what you want and list what you have to give away. You'll be surprised how much of your "junk" your neighbor wants. Appliance parts, old furniture, broken televisions are all snatched up—sometimes in minutes! That nest of wire hangers from the dry cleaners? Yup, those too. Or just take them back to the (organic) dry cleaner next time you drop off some clothes.

Things you thought you couldn't recycle but you can:

- Electronics
- Sneakers
- Batteries
- Motor oil

Begin with a simple Internet search or a phone call to your town office.

Donate food waste to a local garden project or farm. Allow lawn trimmings to naturally fertilize the grass, instead of bagging it and sending a plastic-wrapped bundle of organic material to the landfill.

Reuse plastic and glass containers for home storage. Is a new 12-piece food storage set really necessary? What about those peanut butter jars and yogurt containers? Bring your own bags—plastic, paper, or cloth—when you do your errands; decline new bags whenever possible.

Borrow, rent, or share items used infrequently. Think about sharing lawnmowers and other garden equipment with neighbors. Borrow party decorations and serving pieces from neighbors or rent them. If you live in an apartment building or condo, start a tool "bank." Consider sharing newspaper and magazine subscriptions.

RECYCLE

Lastly, recycle. When possible, choose products made with recycled materials; buy recyclable items and make good on the promise. Most communities now have comprehensive recycling programs. Read and follow the supplied list of what collectors take and what simply fouls up the mix.

Chapter 6

THE GREAT GREEN OUTDOORS

Making the Most of Your Natural Surroundings

IN THE SHORT TIME that the civilized world has populated the planet, our society has gone from a primarily agricultural base to a much more urban/suburban mix. We have sculpted the planet, once a series of harsh habitats, to fit our needs; as the population continues to grow, nature no longer has sufficient resources to provide at our current rate of consumption. By making some adjustments to our daily lives, we can as a whole lessen the burden on the Earth. People can maintain, and even enhance, their environments while also saving money and helping the planet.

Planting Basics

THE RELATIONSHIP BETWEEN PLANTS and animals, developed over millions of years, makes for a fine balance of give and take. Animals (including ourselves) use the oxygen plants respire, we eat the plants and use woody plants, such as trees and bamboo, for raw materials for construction. We, in turn, provide the plants with carbon dioxide and nutrients, both from our bodily wastes and when we decompose.

With this simple knowledge, it's easy to see the benefit of having plants in the house. Fresh air, fresh vegetables, fresh herbs! You can grow some plants indoors year-round. Home gardens also provide a means to reduce organic waste (by composting) and save money at the local market by harvesting your own fresh produce.

Plants use sunlight and carbon dioxide to grow leaves. Their roots in the soil absorb nutrients, including nitrogen, and minerals, such as magnesium and iron. All of these nutrients and minerals are dissolved in water for absorption.

In the garden, the greenhouse, and even on the windowsill, growing your own herbs, fruits, and leafy greens is a healthy and cost-efficient way to eat green. Popular methods of growing your own include hydroponic and aeroponic gardening and the Hortuba table, which allows you to grow fresh veggies with just one square meter of space. You'll be growing basil, rosemary, tomatoes, lettuce, cucumbers, and raspberries in no time!

Old galoshes make original, fun, and earth-friendly flowerpots.

PLANTING INDOORS

Indoor plants enhance any home. They provide fresh air in the house,

Romaine lettuce, low-calorie and high-nutrition, makes a great plant for a small plot.

and also are an attractive and soothing decoration. Many people prefer imported exotic plants, but any seedling can be grown in the home for little money. You don't even need to go to the local hardware store and buy planters, pots, or much of anything thing else. All of it can be acquired for free with a little imagination.

Store-bought pots hold soil and allow for drainage, but there are things lying around the house that you could substitute for them. An old rubber boot with a leak just needs a few more holes (for drainage) to find new life as a pot. Just about any container, from a cracked teapot to a cleaned-out waxed Chinese food takeout box to a cut-down gallon milk jug, are potential flowerpots. Recycle and give a plant a home. With a nail or other thin sharp object, poke 6 to 12 holes in the bottom of the container for any excess water to drain.

PLANT CLIPPINGS

If a friend has a plant that you like, you can ask for a cutting or clipping (several species of plants will simply generate roots at the cut site when placed in moist soil or even water). Good plant maintenance involves pruning, so this can be a win-win situation: your friend shares his or her clippings with you, keeping the parent plant healthy, and you get the chance to create low-cost vegetation.

EASY-ROOTING PLANTS

African violet	Avocado	Basil	Begonia
Carrot	Ficus	Gardenia	Geranium
Honeysuckle	Hydrangea	Jasmine	Mint
Oleander	Petunia	Spider plant	Willow

Place clippings or prunings of these plants in a small container in water, and you'll soon have a plant to root.

Planting and Maintaining an Indoor Herb Garden

▲ Love the taste of fresh herbs? Many of them can be grown indoors or outdoors in minuscule garden plots. A member of the sunflower family, tarragon grows best in full sunlight.

▶ Healthful herbs are known for their high level of antioxidants, with Greek oregano topping the list.

MOST POPULAR HERBS

Fresh herbs help enhance any meal. If you're looking to create a basic kitchen herb garden, consider:

- Basil
- Mint
- Rosemary
- Dill
- Oregano
- Thyme
- Chives
- Parsley
- Sage

Other cooking herbs you may want to try:

- Anise
- Lemongrass
- Bay leaf
- Mustard
- Chervil
- Savory
- Cilantro/Coriander
- Sweet Marjoram
- Garlic Chives
- Tarragon

HERB

GREEK OREGANO
PERENNIAL
Pungent flavor. Use fresh, dried in beef.

HERBS ARE PROBABLY THE MOST COMMON indoor plants, and are quite useful in the kitchen for favorite recipes or herbal teas. Sage, thyme, oregano, and rosemary are everyday household herbs that can be grown easily year-round in the house. Lemongrass, chamomile, and other herbs require a little more work to grow indoors, but it is possible.

The easy herbs listed above do not require much soil, so their pots do not have to be deep; however, the pots should provide a fair amount of surface area for sunlight. Thyme, in particular, has roots that only penetrate about an inch below the soil, yet grows onto a nice healthy bush fairly rapidly. Plants like rosemary and sage grow relative to the amount of soil provided, and these can grow very large if planted outside. An indoor plant, however, provides sufficient leaves to spice up any meal.

Peppermint and Chamomile have both been treasured for centuries. Peppermint is recommended to aid digestion or help an upset stomach, while chamomile has been used as a soothing nighttime beverage to aid sleep.

The flowering tops of the versatile chamomile can be used to a make a soothing and tasty tea for various ailments.

Because plants need only water, soil, and sunlight to survive, growing the plants on your windowsill is fun and easy. If you don't get a lot of light, natural sunlight fluorescent lights are available. In cold climates, make sure the plants are far away enough from the windows so that they don't freeze.

To begin, prepare a pot, cutting small holes for drainage. Place a few pebbles on the pot bottom first (also allowing for drainage), then the soil. If planting from seed, follow the directions provided on seed packets for appropriate depths, although the general rule of thumb for planting depth is four times the width of the seed. After planting the seed, place in a warm place; warmth promotes seed germination. Water once or twice a week, or—in dry climates—three times weekly.

PLANTING TIPS

Prepare the ground: When planting from seeds, the soil should be damp (not wet) prior to planting. Do not place a seed in dry soil and then add water; if the soil is too wet, the seed might rot.

Rotate: Turn your plant a quarter-way around once a week. Plants grow toward sunlight. Rotating will form a nice rounded plant, instead of a plant leaning toward one side.

Prune your plant: Trimming the tips of plants will make them grow bushier. Every tip will yield a "V." After a few weeks, trim the V. For thyme and oregano, especially, this will increase yield.

Dried rosemary

Composting

COMPOST IS ORGANIC MATERIAL used either alone, as a medium to grow plants, or as a soil supplement. The act of composting is the piling of organic materials outdoors to decay, providing nutrient-rich material for the soil. Materials appropriate for composting include all organic kitchen waste, fallen tree leaves, and nontoxic yard trimmings.

All composting requires three basic ingredients:

Browns: Includes materials such as dead leaves, branches, and twigs

Greens: Includes materials such as grass clippings, vegetable waste, fruit scraps, and coffee grounds

Water: Can be tap, gray water, or rainwater

Having the right amount of greens, browns, and water is important. Ideally, a compost pile should have an equal amount of browns to greens and alternate layers of organic materials of different-size particles. The brown materials provide carbon, the green materials supply nitrogen, and the water helps break down the organic matter.

COMPOST DO'S AND DON'TS

What to compost:

- Cardboard rolls
- Clean paper
- Coffee grounds and filters
- Cotton rags
- Dryer and vacuum cleaner lint
- Eggshells
- Farm animal manure
- Fireplace ashes
- Fruits and vegetables
- Grass clippings
- Hair and fur
- Hay and straw
- Houseplants
- Leaves
- Nut shells
- Sawdust
- Shredded newspaper
- Tea bags
- Wood chips
- Wool rags
- Yard trimmings

Think again before you compost:

- Black walnut tree leaves or twigs *(release substances that could harm plants)*
- Coal or charcoal ash *(might contain substances that harm plants)*
- Dairy products, such as butter, egg yolks, milk, sour cream, yogurt *(create odor and attract pests)*
- Diseased or insect-ridden plants *(contaminates compost, spreading disease/insects)*
- Fats, grease, lard, or oils *(create odor and attract pests)*
- Meat or fish bones and scraps *(create odor and attract pests)*
- Pet wastes, such as dog or cat feces, soiled cat litter *(may have harmful parasites, bacteria, germs, pathogens, or viruses)*
- Yard trimmings treated with chemical pesticides *(might kill beneficial composting organisms)*

Source: EPA, September 2007

There is no one "right" way to compost, but you may want to try this approach, as recommended in *A Green Guide to Yard Waste*:

1. Select a dry, shady spot near a water source for your compost pile or bin.
2. Before adding your brown and green materials, be sure to chop or shred larger pieces.
3. Cover your composting area with a 6-inch layer of brown materials.
4. Add a 3-inch layer of green materials and a little soil or finished compost.
5. Lightly mix the two layers above.
6. Top with a 3-inch layer of brown materials, adding water until moist.
7. Turn your compost pile every week or two with a pitchfork to distribute air and moisture. Move the dry materials from the edges into the middle of the pile. Continue this practice until the pile does not reheat much after turning.
8. Your compost will be ready in one to four months, but let the pile sit for two weeks before using.

Composting can significantly cut down on landfill, 23 percent of which consists of yard trimmings and food waste.

Worm Castings: Natural Fertilizer

When red worms are placed in bins with organic matter, they break down the matter into a high-value compost called castings. This form of composting, called vermicomposting, has only a few basic requirements, among them: worms, worm bedding (shredded newspaper, cardboard), and a bin to contain the worms and organic matter. Maintenance includes preparing bedding, burying garbage, and separating worms from their castings. Worms are sensitive to variations in climate so do not expose them to extreme temperatures or direct sunlight. Optimal temperatures for vermicomposting range from 55°F to 77°F. In hot, arid areas, place the bin in the shade or vermicompost indoors. The main thing is to keep the worms alive and healthy by giving them the proper conditions and enough food.

One pound of mature worms (approximately 800–1,000 worms) can eat up to half a pound of organic material a day. It typically takes three to four months for worms to produce harvestable castings that are usable as potting soil. Vermicomposting also produces compost or "worm" tea, a high-quality liquid fertilizer for houseplants or gardens. If this sounds too difficult, you can go the easy route and buy Terracycle, which provides you with a recycled drink bottle full of liquefied worm castings.

Growing Fresh Vegetables and Fruits

Tomatoes are some of the easiest vegetables to grow and can be raised in a garden, window box, or flowerpot.

AS FOOD COSTS RISE, it makes more sense than ever to consider growing your own fresh vegetables and fruits. As an added benefit, home-grown produce often tastes noticeably better than store-bought varieties, and gardeners can avoid the chemical pesticides and herbicides commonly used by commercial growers.

In addition, your garden-raised produce is right outside the door. Instead of having to drive to a grocery store to pick up a few tomatoes, you can simply walk out to the yard and pluck a few at the peak of their flavor. If your garden provides a surplus, you can also freeze or can the remaining produce for a healthy, flavorful, and very cost-effective winter treat.

To grow a successful fruit and vegetable garden, planning is imperative.

Don't overdo it: It may be tempting, but don't go overboard on the size of a beginning garden. Even a 4-foot-by-4-foot garden can yield a good variety of fruits and vegetables that will help reduce your food bill. People without yard space can also get a nice harvest through a container garden.

Be a picky planter: Select fruits and vegetables that you already eat, rather than plants that you think should be in a garden. In other words, grow broccoli if you know you will eat it, not because you think you should.

Be cost-effective: Choose fruits and vegetables that provide the most bang for the buck. Some fruits and vegetables are particularly high in economic value based on how long they need to grow, how much they produce, and how expensive comparable produce would be at a grocery store. Those with high homegrown value include beets, onions, carrots, cucumbers, green beans, leaf lettuce, pea pods, peppers, snap peas, heavy-producing summer squash, and tomatoes. Fruits and vegetables with lower homegrown value include watermelon, cantaloupe, other melons, corn, pumpkins, and winter squash. Besides these annual crops, perennial crops are often worthwhile economically. These include asparagus, horseradish, strawberries, grapes, and rhubarb, as well as some kitchen herbs, such as thyme, basil, and oregano.

Why buy costly and quick-to-wilt commercial herbs, when even a tiny plot yields plenty of fresh greens?

Jump start your growing season by starting your seedlings indoors. Be sure to rotate them; they will bend toward the sun.

Mind your growing season: Once you have decided what you would like to grow, determine whether you will be planting from seed, which is the cheaper alternative, or from purchased transplants. Seeds are a good choice if the plants will mature in the growing window for your area. Gardeners in cool climates can grow such vegetables as lettuce, peas, beans, zucchini, and carrots from seed sown right in the garden, but would do better with transplants of peppers, tomatoes, and Brussels sprouts that require a longer season to harvest. Of course, gardeners can also start many long-season plants from seeds indoors well before the growing season begins, and generate their own transplants.

Save your seeds: Seed packets contain dozens of seeds, and most backyard gardens do not need that many plants. Fortunately, you can store leftover seeds in airtight containers in the refrigerator, where they will last for several

NATURAL PEST CONTROL

One way to deal with pesky critters invading your home turf is to fight bad bugs with good ones. These beneficial insects protect your plants by eating the parasites that eat your garden.

Green lacewing: Eats aphids, mealy bugs, moth eggs, scales, spider mites, thrips, white flies

Hypoaspis mite: Eats fungus gnats, springtails, thrips pupae

Ladybug: Eats alfalfa weevils, aphids, asparagus beetle larvae, chinch bugs, mites, thrips, whitefly

Minute pirate bug: Eats aphids, caterpillars, mites, thrips

Red scale parasite: Eats ivy scale, oleander scale, various red scales, yellow scale

Praying mantid: Eats aphids, beetles, caterpillars, grasshoppers, leaf hoppers, mites

years. To test whether they are still viable, roll some of the seeds in a wet paper towel, set the towel in a plastic bag on a counter for 5 to 10 days, and check the seeds for sprouts. You can also plant these sprouts to give your seedlings a head start in the garden.

If you're going to save your seeds, remember to label their packets so that you can identify them later.

Energy-Efficient Landscaping

THE MOST ENERGY-EFFICIENT LANDSCAPING plans are not only earth friendly but can also save considerable money on both your winter and summer energy bills. The U.S. Department of Energy (DOE) estimates that a landscape designed for energy efficiency will return the initial investment in just eight years. By planting native varieties of flowers, shrubs, and trees, carefully selecting their location in the yard, and taking into account their maintenance, water, and other requirements, you can design your yard to benefit the planet, as well as your pocketbook.

GO NATIVE

Selecting plants that are native to your area makes sense on several fronts:

- Once established—usually with a minimum of soil preparation and a few weeks of watering—native plants typically need much less care than non-native plants. Native perennials and biennials can survive winter conditions and will return from year to year on their own, and native annuals usually reseed themselves. Plus all of these native plants require little in the way of watering, mulching, or frost protection because they are already well suited to the local climate.

Studies have shown that native plants require less care for the homeowner and are better for the environment.

Enjoy the view and leave the lawn mower in the shed; plant a crop of native wildflowers in a corner of your backyard.

- Non-native plants are sometimes invasive species that can take over a yard if they aren't constantly contained. Yet even the most careful attention from a homeowner may not be enough. Invasive plants frequently spread from gardens to natural areas, where they will also threaten native plant communities.

- Unlike a monoculture of Kentucky bluegrass or other lawn, a yard strewn with native wildflowers and grasses needs no mowing—and therefore no mowing-related fuel—and little if any care. As an added benefit, a diverse and native-planted yard provides habitat for often-beneficial insects, birds, and other wildlife; its comparatively deeper roots provide natural erosion control and prevent runoff. And it's quite attractive.

- Native plants have a natural place in the local ecosystem. Local insects and plants have evolved together and often even depend on one another; many native plants need native insects for pollination, and many insects rely on nectar for food. Native plants also have inherent defenses against damage from native insects, while non-native plants often need repeated applications of pesticides to keep insect damage at bay and are more susceptible to naturally occurring plant diseases.

Deciduous trees, which shed their leaves every autumn, provide cooling shade in summer and allow for natural lighting in winter.

TAKE ADVANTAGE OF SHADE

Almost everyone enjoys taking a break from the hot summer sun under a leafy shade tree, but some of us often overlook the large energy benefits of a well-placed tree in our backyard landscaping. According to the DOE, the temperature beneath a shade tree can dip up to 9° F lower than the surrounding, unshaded air and a full 25° F lower than that above a nearby blacktop driveway.

MAKING THE MOST OF SHADE

Consider the sun: Place trees on the south and west sides of a house where they can shade walls, windows, and—when they grow tall enough—the roof.

Shade your AC: Situate a tree near an air conditioner. The DOE estimates that a shaded air conditioner runs about 10 percent more efficiently than one that sits in the sun.

Cool your walkways: Surround patios and sidewalks near the house with hedges or other plants. Their shade will help keep the pavement cooler, and therefore lessen the radiation of the pavement's heat to the house. Be sure, however, to choose shrubs that match your specific needs. For example, evergreen shrubs provide shade year-round, but it might not be a good choice to enclose a patio if their foliage is so dense that it also blocks all cooling breezes in the summer.

Provide infrastructure: Consider a pergola or trellis with a climbing vine to shade a patio or porch.

Work with the weather: Remember your climate when choosing a shade tree. In northern temperate climates, for instance, deciduous trees make sense because they provide shading in the heat of the summer and also lose their leaves during the winter to allow the house to gain at least some heat from the winter sun.

Think about the future: When selecting a tree, think about its growing time and its shape. Some trees, such as aspens, grow much more quickly than others, such as oaks. Oaks, however, generally live much longer, grow considerably taller, and ultimately shade better because they have denser foliage and a broader crown shape. Some homeowners opt for a combination of fast- and slow-growing trees.

CURB THE WIND

A summer breeze can be highly appreciated in the heat of summer, but during a cold winter, the north wind is rarely welcomed. A well-positioned windbreak, however, can keep the winter wind from rattling and penetrating windows and help cut back on heating costs.

- Because winter winds typically come from the north to northwest, most people plant their windbreaks on those sides of a house. Windbreaks should not, however, be planted too closely to the home. To gain the most advantage, experts recommend planting windbreak trees at a distance from the house of between two and four or five times their height when full-grown.

- For windbreak trees, consider planting sturdy evergreens that have branches all the way to ground level. These trees keep their leaves all year, making them good year-round windbreaks, and also block wind just above the Earth's surface and at the heights.

- If you already have some well-positioned, windbreak trees that have high crowns but no lower-level branches, think about adding evergreen shrubs that can fill the gaps. Besides blocking the wind, the shrubs can also hinder blowing snow that would otherwise sweep against the house and over walkways.

CUT YOUR WATER USAGE

To be planet-conscious and to save on utility costs, use water sparingly. Your yard is a good place to start; an estimated 30 percent of all residential water goes toward landscape maintenance. Some tips to save water in the yard include:

Evergreens with foliage from top to bottom make efficient windbreaks. Trees that block the wind can reduce the cost of heating and cooling by up to 20 percent.

Climbing vines trailing over a pergola create a cooling canopy for a backyard oasis from the summer sunshine.

Water early: Temperatures are usually lower in the morning. In the early hours of the day, less water will evaporate away before it gets into the ground and to your plants.

Drip irrigate: Install soaker hoses or a drip irrigation system. In both cases, water seeps out slowly and right into the ground where it will do the most good for your plants. In comparison, water from traditional sprinklers is far more prone to evaporation and runoff.

Choose native stock: Select plants that do well in your conditions. Many climates, even northern climates, have hot and arid summers. By choosing plants that can survive heat and drought, you can keep watering to a minimum. Many native plants are both heat- and drought-tolerant.

Group plants: Plant species that have similar requirements—such as those that need moister conditions—near one another so that you have less area to water.

Be site-specific: Place drought-loving plants along driveways and other sloping areas, so you don't have to water in these locations where water is more likely to be wasted as runoff.

Add mulch: This keeps the soil cooler and prevents soil-level evaporation.

Keep Your Pool Clean and Green

You know what happens after swimming in a chlorinated pool. Your eyes are a bit irritated. Your skin and hair feel dry and smell nasty. Your swimsuit starts to lose its color too (chlorine, after all, is a component of bleach). Your pool liner is slowly breaking down as well. If the chlorine is damaging the liner of your pool, imagine what it's doing to your skin!

Of course, you wouldn't feel so great if you were swimming in a pool full of microorganisms and bacteria, either. Chlorine is very effective at killing the biological soup that grows in every swimming pool. But in some forms, it could actually kill you.

As the chloride ion, chlorine is part of table salt. But in its common elemental form, chlorine is a poisonous pale green gas. Chlorine properly added to swimming pool water is at low concentrations and will not kill you. The real hazard is for the person adding the chlorine to the pool. When you open a container of chlorine, breathing in the gas that has built up under the lid can knock you out. Undiluted chlorine is a skin irritant, handle it with

Save Water Too

Install a pool cover to prevent evaporation. This can save hundreds of gallons of water a month and will also reduce heating and chemical bills.

- Reduce splashing—or at least, the very big splashes that spray water onto the deck and lawn.
- Plug in the overflow line when you're using the pool.
- Use a broom when cleaning around the pool, not a hose.
- Turn off the tile spray device on your automatic pool cleaning equipment.
- Backwash only as often as necessary. Some pool filters do not have to be backwashed; you can take them apart and clean them.

HOW CAN YOU MAINTAIN YOUR SWIMMING POOL?

METHOD	DESCRIPTION	EFFECTIVENESS	TOXICITY	STARTUP COST	ANNUAL COST	SIDE EFFECTS
Chlorine	green-yellow, odors	high	high	medium	medium	burning eyes, irritated skin, damaged hair
Bromine	reddish brown, smelly	high	medium	medium	medium	irritated skin
Hydrogen peroxide	odors	low	medium-low	high	very high	eye irritation
Ozone	gas	medium-low	low	high	high	removes dissolved metals, soaps, oils; not effective on algae
Salt water	salt granules	high	low	high	low	good for skin, prevents infection
Copper ionization	clear	high	low	medium	very low	none

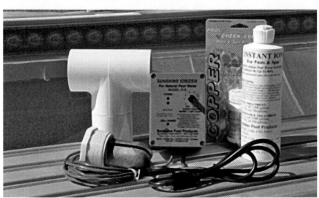

care. Never mix chlorine with anything else—algaecides, alkalis, acids, and other chemicals, when mixed with chlorine, can burst into flames.

Chlorine gas can also gather on the pool's surface as the chemical breaks down, irritating the delicate lining of your nose and even your lungs. Splash-off and runoff from pools leeches chlorine into the environment. And in the upper atmosphere, chlorine-containing molecules have been implicated in the destruction of the ozone layer.

The good news is that chlorine is not your only option. You can have a clean, clear, safe pool without using toxic chemicals.

▲ Although you will initially need a considerable amount of salt (about 100 pounds for a 4,000-gallon pool), salt doesn't evaporate, so replenishment will be minimal.

◄ Copper-silver ionization purifies water by inhibiting algae growth and killing bacteria and viruses. Every purifier includes a test kit that can measure the amount of copper ions in the water. Test once a week during hot summer months.

Chapter 7

BUYING LOCAL

Healthful and Appealing Options

THE BEST WAY TO EAT sustainably is to buy locally. The average supermarket offers food that's been on the road a long time. The average American foodstuff burns unnecessary energy by traveling 1,500 miles from the farm to the table.

Buying local food helps not only the environment but also the palate. Most people don't realize that what's sacrificed by shipping food from far away is what we value most: taste. Take the egg. Most supermarket eggs have flimsy whites and pale yellow yolks, reflecting the substandard diet of the factory-raised chickens. Chickens that feed naturally on bugs and grasses are healthier. The nutrient-rich yolk of a locally raised egg is bright orange. When fried, it "stands up" in the pan, as chefs in the know say. Plus, because local eggs are fresher, they'll last longer in your fridge.

The Environmental Cost of Moving Food

EVERY STEP OF INDUSTRIAL FARMING gobbles up nonrenewable fuels like oil and coal. When these fuels are burned, they pollute the water we drink and air we breathe.

**Buying locally =
Better-tasting food + Less pollution!**

Did you know that roughly one-third of the world's greenhouse gasses are the result of food production? Animal agriculture alone accounts for one-fifth of carbon accumulation worldwide.

LARGE-SCALE WASTE

The greatest energy use in commercial agriculture is the production of chemicals, such as petroleum-based fertilizer. Most animals and crops raised in the United States are done so on a large scale. Growing only one crop on thousands of acres leeches nutrients from the soil without putting anything back, requiring more fertilizer every year. An average of 5.5 gallons of fossil fuels are used on every acre of crops. Reducing the repetitive application of fertilizer on 250 million acres of American cropland would conserve $1 billion worth of fuel. Large-scale farming relies on diesel-fueled tractors and harvesting equipment.

Commercial fertilizer is used to grow grain for factory-fed cows, pigs, and chickens. This grain is then trucked hundreds, sometimes thousands, of miles to factory farms. Animal waste must then be trucked out. These industrial farms also require fuel-hungry machines to feed the animals and ventilate buildings.

▲ Industrial-scale farming relies on vast acreages to produce single crops. The result? Depleted nutrients in once-fertile soil, which eventually spells lower productivity and higher costs.

▼ Just one town in California's San Joaquin Valley produces most of the asparagus consumed in the entire United States.

Industrial-scale farming has also altered entire regions of the country. The plains have become the Wheat Belt, while much of the Midwest is devoted to corn and soybeans. California's San Joaquin Valley supplies approximately 90 percent of all fresh vegetables eaten in the United States. The concentration of farms means longer distances to distribution centers and stores. Although most Americans live within 20 miles of farm-raised broccoli, the average head of supermarket broccoli has traveled 1,800 miles.

SMALL-FARM EFFICIENCY

Compare this fuel use with that of a traditional small farm. Pasture-raised animals feed themselves on grass and distribute their own fertilizer to regenerate the soil. Many small-scale farmers practice no-till agriculture, a soil conservation method in which no tractors are needed. These farms need only rain, sun, and wind.

PACKAGING, TRANSPORTING, AND STORING FOOD

Packaging and storing food is another waste of energy. Instead of buying that can of corn at the supermarket, consider getting local corn and freezing it yourself. Freezing is easy and preserves freshness better than manufacturers' canning.

Buying locally raised fruit, vegetables, dairy, and meat products dramatically cuts down on the use of fossil fuels. It makes sense: buying food grown closer to you decreases the fuel needed to put it on your table. Small farms use significantly less chemical fertilizer through the age-old techniques of crop rotation and composting, turning waste into plant food. For this reason small farms are also much more cost efficient.

A community or allotment garden, such as this one in Seattle, Washington, gives urban dwellers a chance to grow their own fruits and vegetables.

What you can do: visit your local farmers market or join a Community Supported Agriculture (CSA) project. Investing in local farms feeds more people healthier food. Keeping these farms alive preserves land and coveted bucolic views. City dwellers, look around you. Locally produced food may be closer than you think. Urban gardens are gaining in popularity. Even in New York City, one man maintains rooftop beehives from which he harvests truly local honey.

Also remember that as with people, food that travels long distances gets tired. Lettuce wilts; asparagus droops. Fruit is picked green so that it doesn't spoil during the voyage. Unripe fruit is mealy and tasteless—hardly worth the energy needed to eat it, never mind produce it.

Shopping Green

Farmers' Market Tips

- Bring cash, including some smaller bills.
- Get there early for the best selection; sellers sometimes run out.
- Ask for cooking recommendations.
- Bring more than one bag; you don't want the apple-cider doughnuts mingling with the onions.
- Try the samples; you might just find your new favorite!

Buying fruits from local suppliers guarantees freshness and flavor unavailable in imported produce.

BEING A GREEN SHOPPER can feel overwhelming at first, but a few easy adjustments will make a big difference. In no time you'll find yourself reducing waste and eating better.

Food writer Michael Pollan provides a few simple guidelines for navigating the supermarket. These tools will help you fill your shopping cart with better-tasting, fuel-efficient items.

Shop the margins: The most highly processed foods are located in the center aisles of supermarkets. They contain preservatives to lengthen shelf life and help food endure long journeys.

Look for simple ingredients: Don't buy products containing more than five ingredients or ingredients with indecipherable names that you can't pronounce. Each added ingredient means another high-energy process. Whole grains, fruits, and vegetables undergo myriad changes to become that unrecognizable word with lots of *t*'s and *d*'s.

Use your voice: Ask store managers to post signs noting locally grown and organic produce. Talk to the guy or gal at the meat counter. Ask what meats are grass-fed, organic, and come from local farms. If the kind you want is not available, place a request for sustainably raised products, and ask your friends to do the same. Ask where your fish comes from. Is it wild-caught or farm-raised? Was it flown in from Japan or fished off the nearest coast?

Size it up: Buying in bulk is cost-efficient and uses less packaging. Some stores have bulk sections selling grains, nuts, dried fruits, and spices. You take home only what you want and pay by the pound. Instead of three small bags of plastic-packaged rice, fill a recyclable paper bag and store it in a reusable container.

Look for products sold many to a package rather than individually wrapped. For example, if you're a tea drinker, buy loose-leaf instead of a box of paper-wrapped bags, or if you like a tea bag, buy the ones that aren't individually wrapped and don't have a string, tag, or staple (good for microwaving, too).

BYOB: Bring your own bag. Brown-paper grocery bags last for several shopping trips. Cloth totes are sturdy and endlessly reusable. You can often rinse and reuse plastic produce bags. Some supermarkets sell reusable drawstring bags for items like apples and carrots that need less protection. Once a plastic or paper bag has been used to death, recycle it. Many stores have bins near the exit.

▲ Many pantry staples, such as olives, spices, grains, and nuts, are sold in bulk, which keeps both waste and price down.

◄ Don't throw that out! Even paper grocery bags are good for multiple shopping trips.

It may not appear so, but providing new plastic and paper produce and grocery bags is costly for the supermarket. If enough people reuse, customers might see a reduction in prices.

Buy local: Farmers' markets and farm stands don't prepackage their food. Bring your own tote and reusable bags. Let your cucumbers and zucchinis share a bag instead of using one for each. Urban shoppers frequenting farmers' markets can use wheeled carts.

DIY: From-scratch Baking

SOME OF THE MOST TEMPTING products in the supermarket are the packaged baked goods: cookies, snacks, and pancake and brownie mixes. Unfortunately these seemingly appealing foods are highly processed and often wrapped in nonrecyclable plastic. Unhealthy ingredients such as high-fructose corn syrup and hydrogenated oils help preserve these sweets. The good news is that baking from scratch is easy and fun—not to mention delicious.

THE BASICS

Home baking allows you to control the ingredients and avoid tasteless, manufactured preservatives. Buy organic ingredients. Most of what's in those bakery cookies you love—flour, sugar, chocolate, vanilla extract—begin as whole foods that can be grown organically. The basics are also often available in bulk, reducing packaging and cost. Buy the dairy products at the farmers' market; get butter and milk that's antibiotic- and hormone-free. Even better, seek out products from grass-fed cows. Grass-fed animals don't need grain trucked from the

Honey, manufactured by bees, requires little processing, making it a green choice of sweetener. When baking, look over the recipe: can you replace the processed sugar with honey?

Midwestern Corn Belt—grain raised with heavy applications of petroleum-based fertilizers.

Locally grown organic fruit is far tastier than what gets sold in the grocery store and shines in homemade baked goods. Buy extra fruit during the summer and then freeze it or can it for winter muffins, sweet breads, and pies.

A SWEET SURPRISE

Look at the recipe and consider whether honey or maple syrup can replace refined sugar. Organically raised sugar may cut down on pesticides, but large amounts of energy are still needed to produce granules from the harvested cane. Honey and maple syrup require little processing, and you can often buy them in recyclable and reusable glass jars. These examples of nature's sweetness can usually be found at your local farmers' market.

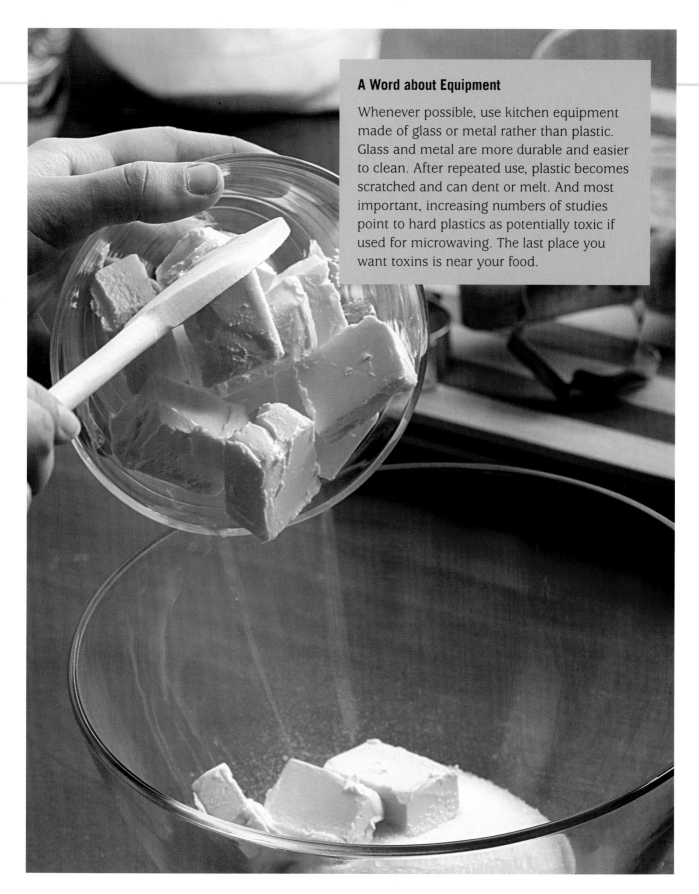

A Word about Equipment

Whenever possible, use kitchen equipment made of glass or metal rather than plastic. Glass and metal are more durable and easier to clean. After repeated use, plastic becomes scratched and can dent or melt. And most important, increasing numbers of studies point to hard plastics as potentially toxic if used for microwaving. The last place you want toxins is near your food.

Green Dining

DINING OUT HAS BECOME one of the great American pastimes—and ordering in a national comfort. We love restaurants and the ease of placing an order or a phone call and having the food appear—voila!—delicious and ready to eat. Eating out comes at the cost of control, though. We don't know what ingredients are used, or if our favorite restaurant recycles their trash. Restaurants are also big consumers of energy—from trucking in food to continually running dishwashers.

Here are a few things you should consider when deciding where to eat.

Look for local, market-based menus: This is good for the planet—less fossil fuel burned flying food to your table—and a great benefit for the farmer. Many small farms are kept in business through

> "Eating well gives a spectacular joy to life and contributes immensely to goodwill and happy companionship."
>
> —Elsa Schiaparelli

Spare the environment and your waistline. Instead of a doggie bag for restaurant leftovers, share a plate.

the large quantities purchased by local chefs. Often this locally grown feature is advertised on a restaurant's menu, Web site, or other promotional material. If not, don't be shy; ask if the hamburger is organic or grass-fed, or where the salad greens come from. The more customers that ask the question, the more likely your favorite joint will consider local options.

Fill out a comment card: Many restaurants leave comment cards or survey forms for their customers to fill out. Be sure to note your preferences for local and organic ingredients. Or if you're on friendly terms with an establishment, ask the owner or manager to switch to napkins and paper towels made from recycled materials. Other questions to ask: are they a member of the Green Restaurant Association, an organization helping the industry use less fuel and create less waste. What do they do with their organic waste? Could what the food patrons don't eat be donated to a local soup kitchen?

Say NO to polystyrene foam: When ordering in, one of the biggest problems is the disposables. Some of this waste can be avoided. If you're picking up food to take home, tell the takeout place you don't want any polystyrene foam, and you don't need napkins, utensils, or those little condiment packets. If your cashew chicken is delivered in a plastic container, don't throw it away. Many of these are sturdy, Tupperware-like dishes you can use to carry your lunch to work. Recycle the paper bags in which your food arrived.

A Note about Those Reuseables

Check labels. Buy products made without Bisphenol-A (BPA), a dangerous chemical that's a common ingredient in hard plastics.

Eat Your Leftovers

It's a bummer when yummy food goes bad because you pushed it to the back of the fridge and forgot about it. Either stick the receipt or label to the refrigerator door, or write yourself a reminder (and put it where you will see it) that there is some good eating to be had with very little effort. If you know that what you bring home from the restaurant, after a detour to the fridge, will ultimately end up in the trash, some plate sharing or appetizer ordering (in place of a main course) might eliminate the leftover dilemma as well as some unpleasant refrigerator odors.

Coffee, Tea, and Other Beverages

Drink organic: Coffee and tea are mostly raised in far-off places like Nicaragua, Kenya, and China, but not all crops are raised equally. Organically raised coffee and tea not only means pesticide-free beans and leaves but also spares workers from harmful toxins. Drink local when you can. Patronize cafes that roast their own beans and make their cappuccinos with hormone-free milk from a local farm. Suggest that managers replace sugar packets with bulk sugar and offer the option of honey.

BYO mug: Bring your own insulated travel mug. Many cafes will offer you a discount. You're doing everyone a service: you save the cafe money on paper cups and keep paper cups (which are often lined with a petroleum-based product) out of the trash bins.

HOW YOUR BEVERAGES ARE MADE, packaged, and transported is just as important as the processing of your food. You can be a more responsible drinker, starting at home.

For starters, drink tap water. In the United States, tap water is safe, plentiful, and free. If you're worried, have your water tested by a local agency, or use a water filter on your tap or one of those systems for your fridge. Those plastic bottles and gallons of drinking water should be kept for emergencies (like losing power) and when you're on the go and can't find a fountain to refill your reusable container.

Need a shot of caffeine in the morning? Whether your preference is coffee or tea, you have eco-friendly options.

▲ Look for organically grown free-trade beans for your morning cup of coffee. Grind the beans yourself for a fresh flavor.

▶ Instead of bags, buy tea in loose leaves. Pour hot water directly over the leaves, or buy an infuser to strain the brew.

Don't buy bleached filters: If you brew your morning beverage at home, consider a coffee maker with a built-in gold filter. Invest in a tea infuser for steeping delicious pots of loose-leaf tea. If you do rely on filters and tea bags, look for unbleached and biodegradable ones.

Microbrews Are Better

Forget that watery stuff that people from other lands term "American" beer. Across the country—from Roots Organic Brewery in Portland, Oregon, to Orlando Brewing in Florida to Brooklyn Brewery in New York City—microbreweries have come into their own. Now that the United States boasts around 1,500 microbreweries, chances are good that there's a microbrewery in your state if not your nearest city.

To locate your closest microbrewery, go to: http://www.real-beer.com/ or http://beeradvocate.com/beerfly/directory/0/US

LIBATIONS

Wine and beer, considered necessities for many of us, can be ecologically tricky. Glass bottles are heavy and therefore use more fuel to transport. Though grapes can't be grown everywhere, look for vintners closer to home. Fortunately, many wineries are beginning earth-friendly biodynamic and organic practices and advertise this on their labels.

Unlike wine, beer can be made almost anywhere. The microbrew phenomenon has been going strong for several years now. Do your part to continue that trend, and sample some regional and original craft beer. Usually transported in kegs, local brews use less glass and metal for bottles and cans.

Why order a beer or ale in a can or bottle, when you can have a frosty glass pulled fresh from the tap? Be sure to sample increasingly available locally brewed beers.

Chapter 8

HOW GREEN IS YOUR RIDE?

Making the Most of Your Wheels

IF YOU'RE IN THE MARKET for a new car, the wide variety of new hybrids matches almost any need. Fuel-efficient hybrids get better mileage than their conventional counterparts, and they have cleaner emissions. If a hybrid is not in your future, try to get the greatest miles per gallon (MPG) out of your current auto. Curious about biodiesel? This clean, veggie-based, carbon-neutral fuel can run in any diesel car or truck with little or no engine modifications. For the more ambitious green driver, straight vegetable oil can make fueling up almost free. Ethanol is another veggie fuel, and there are between 5 and 6 million flex-fuel vehicles already on the road—you may even be driving one and not know it. Whether you drive a hybrid, alternative-fuel, or even a gas-engine vehicle, you can take steps to make your means of transportation more earth-friendly right now.

Car Maintenance Tips for Better Mileage

Improving gasoline mileage is a critical concern, both for the environment and for the typical car owner's budget.

ABOUT 66 PERCENT of all the oil consumed in the United States is used for transportation. Most of that is burned up in the form of gasoline. Luckily, no matter what kind of car you drive, there are things that you can do to improve fuel mileage. Just taking good care of your car will help it reach the gas mileage numbers that the manufacturer promises—and possibly even exceed them.

Get regular tune-ups: Worn spark plugs, dragging brakes, transmission problems, and other routine automotive aches and pains can all have detrimental effects on fuel economy. On average, fixing a car that is noticeably out of tune or has failed an emissions test can improve its gas mileage by about 4 percent.

Replace clogged air filters: This can improve gas mileage by as much as 10 percent.

If it's broke, fix it: Repairing a serious problem, such as a faulty oxygen sensor, can improve your mileage by as much as 40 percent.

Follow directions: Use the grade of motor oil recommended by your car's manufacturer. Using a different motor oil can lower your gas mileage by 1 to 2 percent.

Keep track: Monitor your average fuel economy regularly. If there's a big change, something's wrong with your car. Have it checked out.

Keep your tires pumped: Properly inflated and aligned tires can improve your gas mileage by around 3.3 percent. Buy a tire-pressure gauge, and check your tires every month. The recommended tire pressure is listed in your owner's manual and, usually, on a sticker on the doorjamb of the driver's side door as well. (The "psi" number on the sidewall of the tires is the maximum pressure, not the proper inflation level.)

Use your dipsticks: Check the fluid levels—both oil and transmission fluid—regularly. Your engine will run more efficiently, and you'll head off major break-downs.

Clean out your car: Carrying around your golf clubs or a case of soda in the trunk all the time decreases your gas mileage. Every extra 100 pounds you carry around in your car reduces its gas mileage by 1 to 2 percent.

Keep it clean: Keeping your car washed and waxed improves its aerodynamics. And better aerodynamics translate to better fuel efficiency.

DRIVE SMART TO SAVE GAS

Driving like a maniac is hard on your car. And, as it turns out, it's hard on your planet as well. The choices you make as you drive can have a real impact on the fuel efficiency of your car.

Watch the speed limit: Once you get past about 60 mph, gas mileage drops rapidly. For every five miles per hour that you drive over 65, you get a 7-percent decrease in fuel economy. In areas with traffic lights, driving the speed limit also means fewer red lights, because many signals are timed for optimum traffic flow.

Keep your cool: Aggressive driving wastes gas. Speeding, rapid acceleration, and hard braking can lower your highway gas mileage by a whopping 33 percent and shave 5 percent off your city mileage. Jumping on the accelerator from a stoplight and braking hard just doesn't make sense. Give yourself an extra five minutes to get where you're going, an then keep your trip as smooth and steady as possible.

Choose your cruise control wisely: On the highway cruise control is usually a good idea—but not always. It can improve your gas mileage by helping you maintain a steady speed, but this is only the case when you are driving on mostly flat roads. For a drive through the hills, cruise control will work hard to maintain your set speed, meaning your car will accelerate faster up the hills.

Use the highest gear you can: Cars are designed to start in the lowest gear because that's where they have the most power. But your car's engine speed goes down in higher gear, and that saves gas and

Carpooling

Some people just won't give up their cars and SUVs or don't have feasible, affordable alternatives for getting to work. Although some employers will give a carpool preferential parking or free lunch parties, other benefits include:

Less wear and tear on your car: Sharing the driving duties means that you use your car less, so it is likely to last that much longer.

Lower insurance costs: Some car insurance providers offer lower premiums depending on how often you carpool.

HOV lanes: While single-occupancy vehicles inch along in the regular lanes, you and your compatriot(s) can glide unimpeded down the much-less-crowded high-occupancy vehicle lane. In some areas, HOV lanes allow as few as two people.

Lower costs: By carpooling, commuters use far less gasoline, decreasing smog and other pollution. Also, in some instances, carpoolers pay decreased tolls.

Car Holiday

It doesn't have to be every day. Leaving your car at home and taking mass transit, bicycling, scootering, or tele-commuting just two days a week will reduce the average car's carbon emissions by more than 1,500 pounds a year.

reduces engine wear. If your car has an automatic transmission with a "sport" mode, it's probably designed to keep you in a lower gear longer. This gives you greater performance but decreases your fuel economy.

Use the air conditioning thoughtfully: Running the A/C uses gas, but rolling down your windows makes your car less aerodynamic, which also uses gas. If you're driving slower than about 35 mph, the dif-ference is minuscule; you'll save more gas by roll-ing down the windows. For highway driving, roll up the windows and turn on the air conditioning.

Reduce drag: To transport heavy loads, place items inside the car or trunk, rather than on a roof rack. A loaded roof rack can decrease your fuel econ-omy by 5 percent. Even an unloaded roof rack increases the aerodynamic drag on your car and adds weight. If possible, buy a roof rack that you can remove easily when you don't need it.

Stop idling: Idling your engine gets you 0 miles per gallon. The best way to warm up a car is to drive it. Even on a winter day, you don't need more than

30 seconds of idling. And if you leave your car running while you are wait-ing on line or picking someone up, you're just wasting gas. It's more efficient to turn the engine off while you wait and then restart the car.

Skip the drive-through: Park your car, stretch your legs, and walk into the bank or restaurant.

Combine errands into one trip: Several short trips, each one taken from a cold start, can use twice as much fuel as one trip covering the same distance when the engine is warm. When your engine is cold, it uses more fuel than when it is warm, so combining errands can improve your gas mileage. It might also mean you travel fewer total miles.

Just running a few local errands that keep you off the freeway and your speeds below 35 mph? Rather than cranking up the A/C, roll down the windows and enjoy the refreshing breeze.

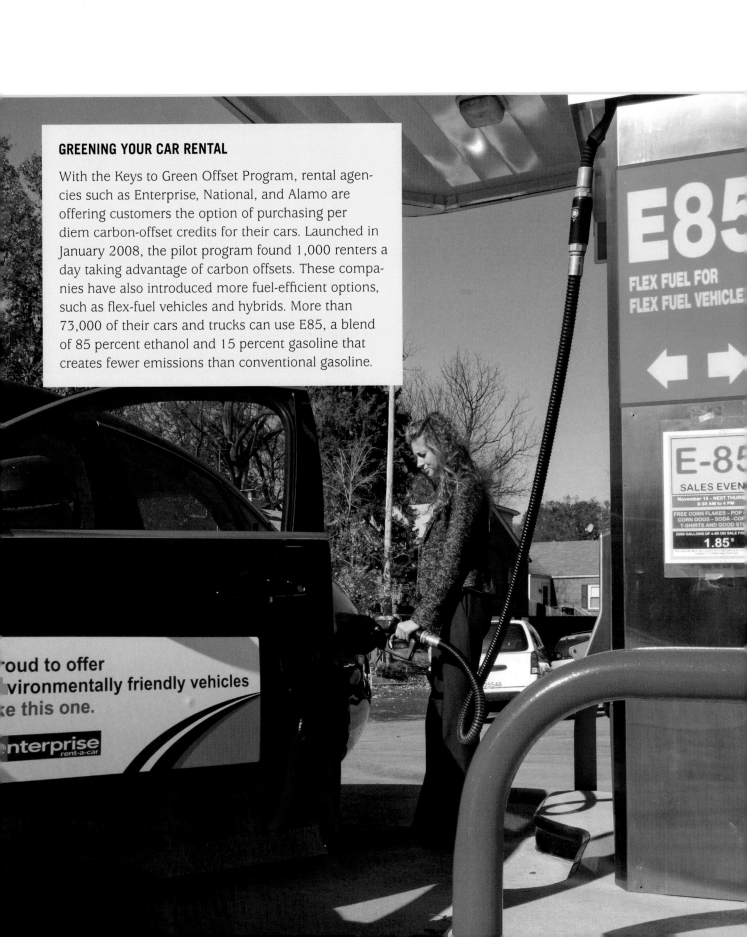

GREENING YOUR CAR RENTAL

With the Keys to Green Offset Program, rental agencies such as Enterprise, National, and Alamo are offering customers the option of purchasing per diem carbon-offset credits for their cars. Launched in January 2008, the pilot program found 1,000 renters a day taking advantage of carbon offsets. These companies have also introduced more fuel-efficient options, such as flex-fuel vehicles and hybrids. More than 73,000 of their cars and trucks can use E85, a blend of 85 percent ethanol and 15 percent gasoline that creates fewer emissions than conventional gasoline.

The New Breed of Autos

HYBRID CARS COMBINE OLD AND NEW TECHNOLOGY for an engine that is more powerful and efficient than either type would be on its own. The old technology is the gasoline-powered internal combustion engine. The new technology is an electric motor, powered by a rechargeable battery. The battery recharges itself by capturing energy that would normally be lost when the car is slowing down or braking. It can also recharge itself by stealing a little power from the gas engine.

Different types of hybrid engines combine these technologies in different ways, which is why hybrid cars offer such wide variations in fuel efficiency. Basically, though, they can all be divided into two categories: mild hybrids and full hybrids.

MILD HYBRIDS VERSUS FULL HYBRIDS

In mild hybrids, the combustion engine drives the car most of the time, and the electric motor helps out with extra power when it's needed. The electric motor cannot work unless the combustion engine is also working.

In full hybrids, the electric motor can sometimes power the car on its own. Often, this happens when the car is driving at

▲ With the electric car's range still limited, some concept cars give drivers several fueling options, including electricity, gasoline, E85, or biodiesel.

▼ Once limited to Toyota and Honda imports, hybrids are now being made by major U.S. auto makers, as well as many others.

Why Buy a Hybrid?

- Hybrid cars save on gas.
- Hybrid owners receive tax breaks
- Hybrids are earth-friendly

◀ Available in many colors and as a hardtop or a convertible, the Smart car became available in the United States in 2008.

▼ Conceived by the CEO of watch manufacturer Swatch, the Smart car was originally nicknamed the "Swatchmobile." "Smart" is an acronym for <u>S</u>watch <u>M</u>ercedes <u>Art</u>.

lower speeds. As the speed picks up, the combustion engine also kicks in and the two work together to power the car.

As a general rule, full hybrids get better gas mileage than mild hybrids. They do especially better in city driving, because the electric motor can often power the car on its own. Both types do, however, use less gas and emit less pollution than internal combustion engines alone.

All hybrids offer another advantage: the federal government and many states offer tax breaks for driving hybrid cars. Many insurance companies offer breaks, too, making for savings in addition to the one at the gas pump.

THE BEST CITY CAR EVER

For city driving—and especially city parking—there's also the new Smart cars. These cars are a joint venture between the makers of the Swatch watch and Daimler, maker of the Mercedes-Benz.

CITY PARKING

Smart cars have a lot of advantages for city drivers, starting with the fact that they are just 8.8 feet long and 5.1 feet wide. That means you can

A Ford Escape hybrid taxi drives the streets of New York City.

park them head-in at the curb, as you would a motorcycle. If you live in a place with nothing but shopping malls and endless parking lots, that may not seem like a big deal. In urban areas, however, where parking spaces are at a premium, and there's invariably a "half-spot" that won't fit your average car, it's almost a dream come true.

SMART AND GREEN

Parking isn't the Smart cars' only advantage either. Smart cars are very green indeed. It starts with the manufacturing process. The cars are put together in Hambach, France, from prefabricated modules made of recycled and recyclable materials. Various eco-friendly painting processes eliminate the need for solvents when adding color, and they consume less energy.

A Smart car has many of the advanced safety and braking features that make the Mercedes-Benz vehicles such reliable rides. And the Smart Fortwo—the two-seater model sold in the United States—is classified as an ultralow-emission vehicle. Although it is still a traditional combustion engine, this baby is no gas guzzler.

Despite its numerous good points, there are still some downsides. The Smart car still doesn't get the same mileage as the best hybrid engines, and the manufacturer recommends using premium unleaded gasoline, which can be especially pricey. (Smart says it's working on all-electric engine models.) Some people find the little car's interior cramped. The three-cylinder engine can be noisy and does not offer great acceleration. And get ready for a sometimes bumpy ride: the car does not cushion the road much.

On the other hand, the Smart car wasn't meant to be opened up on the Autobahn. It's a zip-around-the-city car, with more trunk space and seating than a scooter, plus protection from the elements. Space for groceries, space for a friend, and space to park is an urban dweller's dream.

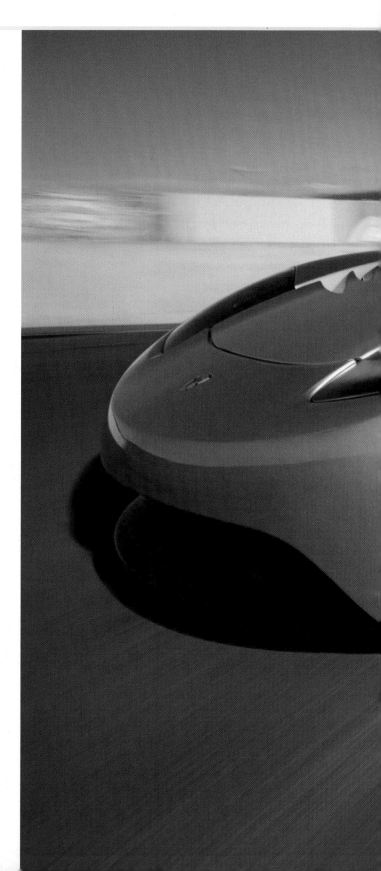

TESLA ROADSTER

Although not yet mass-produced, with any luck, the all-electric Tesla Roadster may be a hint of things to come. With an acceleration of 0 to 60 mph in 3.9 seconds, a sporty, strong, and light carbon-fiber chassis, and an EPA rating of 135 MPG equivalent (remember, it runs on electricity, not gas), this sports car has a lot of get-up-and-go. Of course, top performance and good looks come at a price: its 2008 model (already sold out) is going for a cool hundred grand. Those rich and sufficiently near enough to the top of Tesla Motor's waiting list will be able to go 220 miles between charges with a running cost of approximately two cents a mile.

Alternative Automotive Fuels

AMERICANS USE AUTOMOBILES in almost every aspect of daily life: for work, school, family outings, shopping, recreation, transporting goods, emergency medical transportation, and military purposes. Because there is little likelihood of Americans—or any nationality for that matter—giving up their cars and trucks for the sake of the environment, the next best solution is to power them with cleaner fuels. Ideally, these earth-friendly fuels should be made from renewable sources or recycled materials. Ultimately, their production and combustion should generate a minimum of CO_2 and other greenhouse gases.

Although there are a number of alternative fuels currently being researched—nitrogen and natural gas are two examples—the following fuels are already in use throughout the world.

ETHANOL

The easy-to-manufacture biofuel ethanol (also called grain alcohol) can be made from common crops, such as corn and sugarcane. Already widely used in Brazil, this fuel is quickly becoming an alternative to gasoline in many parts of the world. Currently, most American cars are manufactured to run on a blend with a maximum of 10 percent

Going green may be a lot simpler than you think: check your owner's manual or the inside of your gas tank door to see if your auto takes E85. Some car owners don't even realize that they are driving flex-fuel vehicles.

Protein-rich grains, by-products of the ethanol manufacturing process, can feed both cattle and poultry.

ethanol, but flex-fuel vehicles can run on blends as high as 85 percent ethanol. E85—with 85 percent ethanol and 15 percent gasoline—was created to serve the 6 million flex-fuel vehicles on the road in the United States. Controversy continues about using corn as a source of ethanol. Critics claim that it cuts into the food supply, creating corn shortages and higher prices. Producing ethanol from corn is also six times less efficient than using the tropical crop sugarcane. In terms of the environment, ethanol produces fewer greenhouse gases than gasoline, and although CO_2 is generated during its fermentation and combustion, the amount of CO_2 absorbed by the source crop as it grows offsets this.

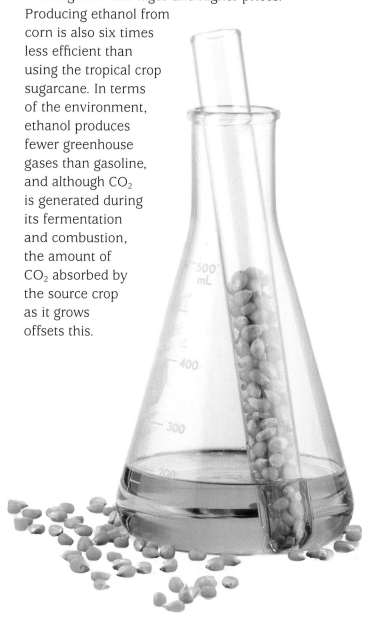

THE ENERGY BALANCE

To produce most biomass fuels—those made from renewable organic matter such as wood, energy crops, and crop residues—the foodstock needs to be grown, collected, dried, fermented, and burned. The amount of energy this process requires, compared to the amount of energy released by combustion of the fuel, is called the energy balance. For instance, one unit of fossil fuel energy is required to produce 1.3 units of energy from corn ethanol. Sugarcane ethanol produces a more efficient 1.8 units of energy.

METHANOL

Methanol, another biofuel, is also known as wood alcohol. Methane gas occurs naturally and is also produced as a by-product of coal mining, landfills, stockyards, and the fossil-fuel industries. Although methane (along with other noncarbon-dioxide emissions) contributes 40 percent to the effects of global warming, methane has potential as an alternative, clean-burning fuel. In the form of compressed natural gas, methane has powered European automobiles, such as Volvos, with carbon dioxide emissions 25 percent lower than those of gas-powered vehicles. Although methane-based cars are a bit more expensive, the cost of fueling them is 20 to 60 percent cheaper than using gasoline or diesel.

HYDROGEN FUEL CELLS

A fuel cell, an electrochemical energy conversion device, produces energy in a way similar to a battery. In a process that converts hydrogen and

WHY USE METHANOL?

Methanol's physical and chemical properties make for an ideal automotive fuel.

Lower pollution: Emissions from methanol-fueled cars cause less smog and other toxic compounds. Trucks and buses that run on methanol emit almost no particulate matter and much less nitrogen oxide than their diesel-fueled counterparts.

More fuel supply options: Methanol can be made from natural gas, wood, or waste pulp, diversifying the U.S. fuel supply and reducing dependence on imported oil.

Better performance: This high-octane fuel offers excellent acceleration and vehicle power.

Economically attractive: With mass production, methanol could be manufactured, distributed, and sold to consumers at prices competitive with gasoline.

Source: EPA, March 2007

FACTS & FIGURES: ALTERNATIVE FUELS

- In 2000 approximately 8 million vehicles worldwide ran on alternative fuels.
- In 1839 Sir William Grove invented a primitive version of the fuel cell called a gas voltaic battery.
- More than 4,000 electric vehicles are operating throughout the United States, with the largest number in California and the western states.
- There are more than 75,000 natural-gas vehicles in the United States, and nearly 1 million worldwide.

oxygen into water, the cell produces electricity quietly, efficiently, and without pollution. Unlike fossil fuels, the by-products of fuel cells are heat and water. A traditional sealed battery stores its chemicals inside and eventually has to be replaced when those chemicals are used up. The chemicals used in a fuel cell, however, constantly flow into the cell so that it never goes dead. There is a major impediment with fuel cells: the hydrogen that they require is created by the electrolysis of water. It would take four times the amount of power presently available on the national grid to create enough hydrogen to power all the cars in the United States. The fuel cell itself requires expensive components, and hydrogen processing also releases hydrocarbons into the atmosphere. Currently, cars that run on fuel cells have short ranges, although the 2008 Honda FCX Clarity is anticipated to have a range of 270 miles.

BIODIESEL

Biodiesel, another biofuel, can be made from a variety of vegetable oils, including soy, corn, rapeseed (canola), cottonseed, peanut, sunflower, avocado, and mustard seed, as well as from recycled cooking oil or animal fats. Despite its name, biodiesel doesn't contain diesel fuel or any other petroleum product. Using biodiesel in a conventional diesel engine substantially reduces emissions of unburned hydrocarbons, nitrated

▲ About 600 fleet vehicles nationwide use biodiesel blends; most diesel engines run on biodiesel without any alterations.

▼ Because it's easier on the engines than gasoline, methanol has fueled all Indianapolis 500 cars for more than thirty years.

polycyclic aromatic hydrocarbons, carbon monoxide, polycyclic aromatic hydrocarbons, sulfates, and particulate matter. In Europe, biodiesel is an accepted substitute for fossil fuels in autos and is also used as heating fuel in some countries. As with ethanol, the greenhouse emissions created from producing biodiesel are offset by the carbon dioxide uptake of the crops grown as foodstock.

The Joy of Scooters

WHEN IT COMES to two-wheeled transportation, most people stop at the bicycle. Sadly, unless ridden by a die-hard cyclist, most bicycles tend to stay in the garage. Commuting or running errands via bike is dusty, sweaty business and doesn't mix well with office attire. And unless your errands involve small, lightweight items, a bike doesn't serve as the best choice for grocery shopping or dropping off dry cleaning. Most places are also not bike friendly enough to be safe for serious cycle transportation. Luckily, a better and remarkably green solution exists: the motor scooter.

Scooters combine the freedom and ease of cycling with the motorized power and greater range of a car. Best of all, scooters get great mileage, work well for quick errands and non-highway commuting, and are easy to park right in front of most stores, restaurants, and movie theaters. Tuck a scooter between two parked cars, and you'll be enjoying your popcorn long before your friends arrive after hunting for a space or hiking from the parking garage. Plus you'll have the added bonus of having fun and looking fashionable.

There are some key benefits to owning a motor scooter, including:

100 miles per gallon: A small scooter (80cc) can zip around town sipping on gasoline to the tune of 100 miles to the gallon. Because they are not designed to operate at highway speed (most scooters top out at about 40–50 mph), a motor scooter makes a great ride for anyone in a city or neighborhood with alternative roadways.

Safer than a bike or motorcycle: The reason is acceleration. A bike depends on the rider's reflexes and speed to avoid a problem. This is hard to do if a car jumps in your path or cuts you off. On the other hand, a motorcycle can reach high speeds—exhilarating to most motorcycle owners but also very dangerous. A scooter gives you enough zip to get away from things but not too much that you're at serious risk. Of course, all two-wheeled vehicles are more dangerous than cars—you are definitely vulnerable, but a scooter is your best bet for two-wheeled safety.

A motor scooter is an economical and practical way of getting around. Far more eco-friendly than a car, a well-tuned scooter usually burns about a gallon of gas every 100 miles.

Errand-running machines: Hard to picture, but a scooter is a pack mule for running errands. Unlike a motorcycle, which offers only a seat over an engine, most scooters have hidden compartments under their seats and ingenious ways to clip grocery bags under the seat latch. Pile the bags on the foot bed and you can transport four or five bags of groceries back from the supermarket without losing an apple. Of course, overloading a scooter is not a good idea if it becomes hard to steer, but most owners are surprised at how much they can haul using locking baskets, under-seat storage, and the floorboard.

No special driver's license needed: In most states a scooter is considered a moped and doesn't require a motorcycle license, so there's no other driving test. A street-legal scooter must be registered, and you must have a valid license, but you can start driving the second you leave the showroom, with no learner's permit or special license required. Best of all, you don't need special insurance on a motor scooter, although modest plans will protect your property from theft.

This rider shows off good scooter form: wearing a helmet, she keeps both hands on the controls and her feet on the floorboards.

Scooter 101

Take a motorcycle or moped safety course: Scooters are not toys. And driving in a city is very risky if you do not have solid command of your vehicle, whether it has two wheels or four. Give yourself plenty of time to practice before riding with regular traffic. Learn how to signal, to make sure other drivers see you, and how to handle turns, steep hills, and sudden stops.

Own your lane: Unlike a bicycle, a scooter is entitled by law to a full lane of the road it travels on. Don't make the common—and hazardous—mistake of many beginner scooter riders: timidly hugging the side of the road. This confuses most drivers, who are unsure if they can pass you. If you are riding very far over, most cars will pass you, making the ride nerve-wracking and downright dangerous. Your position in the lane should make it clear to other drivers that you are in front of them and that they must pass you just as they pass any other car: only when there is a passing lane.

Always look behind you: As a scooter driver, you need to be especially conscious of the traffic following you. Other motor vehicles are likely to being traveling faster than your scooter, so frequently check your mirrors; every five to seven seconds should let you know when a car has come up behind you. Remember, too, that mirrors allow only a partial view to your rear. Be aware of your particular blind spots, and check them often.

Skip the Commute: Go Green with a Home Office

Stay-at-home mom or working mother? These days many women fill both roles simultaneously as increasing numbers of workers—women and men alike—telecommute from home offices.

IN HIS **2007** BOOK, *Microtrends*, pollster Mark Penn estimates that 4.2 million Americans now work exclusively from home (that's almost a 100 percent increase from 1990), and about 20 million are in home offices at least part-time. Some of them are employees in the traditional sense who telecommute, but most are self-employed contract workers, consultants, and freelancers who set themselves up in home work spaces.

Working from home saves energy and time by cutting out the commute. But it ups your home energy consumption—sometimes dramatically.

Here are some questions telecommuters frequently ask about greening their home offices.

Are there energy-saving electronics I can get for my home office?

Yes! Just about anything you plug in comes in an energy-efficient version. Overall, energy-efficient products use about half as much electricity as their electric-hungry counterparts, and some use as much as 90 percent less.

Surrounding yourself with machines also puts a strain on your personal environment. Energy-saving products reduce noise from transformers and fans, making your home workspace quieter. Electromagnetic field emissions are also lower from energy-efficient monitors.

I don't use my printer and fax machine all the time. Do they keep using energy even when they're idle?

They do. Simply turning off any machines you're not using can save a significant amount of energy.

You need to turn them all the way off, however. Many home appliances and electronics, including computers, keep drawing a little bit of power—even when they are switched off. It's not really practical to go around unplugging every single appliance in your home when it's not in use, but it is practical to plug them all into power strips and then switch the power strips off. Cutting off the power means your switched-off office machines won't keep sipping electricity.

What about turning off my computer? I've heard computers last longer if you always leave them on.

That was true back in the days when we needed a mainframe computer to do the work that a single laptop does now. Today's modern computers don't need to be on when they're not working.

HOME-OFFICE NECESSITIES

Look for energy-saving versions when buying:

- Computers
- Monitors
- Copiers
- Fax machines
- Printers
- Scanners
- Cordless phones
- Multifunction devices (such as a fax/scan/copy printer)

How do energy-efficient computers get the savings? Is it from less computing power?

An energy-efficient computer uses 70 percent less electricity, but when it comes to processing power, you're not giving anything away. When they're not using their processing unit, energy-efficient computers enter a low-power mode in which they use 15 watts of power or less. Spending lots of time in low-power mode also helps equipment run cooler and last longer. But remember, the low-power mode is activated automatically only when you turn that feature on. Most come with the power management features activated, but check and make sure.

Do screen savers really save energy?

Nope. Letting the computer automatically switch to sleep mode or manually turning the monitor off is always the better energy-saving strategy.

Which are more energy-efficient, laptops or desktop computers?

Laptops—for the most part. But that is changing. Today's desktop computers with flat-screen technology (the processing unit is incorporated right into the screen housing, as in Apple iMacs) use the same kind of processors that laptops do, and that means they're just as efficient.

To maximize your energy savings with a laptop, plug the AC adapter into a power strip that you can turn off, because the laptop's transformer draws power even when the laptop is not plugged into the adapter.

What about the stuff I don't plug in?

You can save trees and conserve energy by recycling your office paper. Start by simply printing on both sides of every sheet or use the blank backs of printed sheets for scrap paper and note-taking. And if you start out buying recycled paper (about the same price as nonrecycled or even cheaper if you catch it on sale), you can continue and encourage this cycle.

If your community recycles paper, set up a separate receptacle in your home office so you can be sure every bit of paper (even the pages you shred) ends up in the recycling bin.

TELECOMMUTING

With so many means of communication open to the average professional, telecommuting provides a way to put in a full or partial day by working from somewhere other than the usual workplace. Telecommuting is well suited to positions where the employee has no direct contact with the public, and direct contact with co-workers is not required. Employees can be connected to the office via computer, fax, or telephone.

Benefits of Telecommuting

Less congestion: Telecommuting reduces the number of automobile trips employees take into work each week; reducing the number of cars during rush hour also makes commuting safer.

Less pollution: Less driving means reduced pollution, as transportation represents over one-third of carbon dioxide emissions.

Less expensive: No tolls, no car maintenance, no lunch out makes for a low-cost day.

Chapter 9

EARTH-FRIENDLY CHECKLISTS

Guidelines for a Greener Outlook

USE THESE HANDY CHECKLISTS to elevate your green quotient—whether you're building a new house or planting a garden from scratch, undertaking a major home renovation, or simply updating your current house. You'll find guidelines for buying green building products, improving insulation, eliminating moisture, and updating your appliances and electronic devices. You'll be able to follow steps to make your car and driving more earth-friendly, and to turn your workspace, apartment, or dorm room into a haven of green. You'll also discover that these checklists will serve as a springboard, and that before long you'll be coming up with your own ways to save energy, reduce waste, and shrink your carbon footprint both inside and outside your home.

At Home and in the Neighborhood

GENERAL HOME

☐ Insulate, weatherize, and air seal your doors, windows, and pipe entries.

☐ Install energy-efficient heating and cooling systems.

☐ Install programmable thermostats that automatically adjust the temperature based on peak usage.

☐ Insulate your water heater, and turn it down to 120°F.

☐ Consider electricity from a renewable energy source, such as solar panels, or buy it from an approved green-energy provider.

☐ Switch to compact fluorescent light bulbs in high-use areas.

☐ Add natural lighting with additional windows or skylights.

☐ If you live in a part of the country where radon is a problem, check that levels are below 4 picocuries per liter of air (pCi/l).

☐ Make sure there is no asbestos in your older home, or that it has been encapsulated.

☐ Check that there is no fresh-air intake near polluted air sources, such as street traffic, or near any equipment exhaust vents.

☐ If you need to call an exterminator, make sure chlordane (a synthetic chemical that eliminates termites) is not used.

☐ Shop for curtains, upholstery, and other fabrics that are made of natural fibers printed with nontoxic inks.

- ☐ Choose carpeting made from untreated natural fibers, such as cotton or wool.

- ☐ Look for flooring products made from rapidly renewable resources, such as bamboo, cork, or linoleum.

- ☐ Consider installing flooring or wall paneling made of reclaimed wood products or certified wood harvested from sustainably managed forests.

Bedroom

- ☐ Shop for bed frames that do not contain pressed wood or synthetic adhesives.

- ☐ Look for bedding made of cotton and/or wool, not foam or another synthetic.

- ☐ Shop for bed linens made of 100-percent organic cotton.

- ☐ Consider purchasing a green mattress that incorporates natural latex foam.

- ☐ Use pillows filled with nonsynthetic materials or recycled polyester.

Kitchen

- ☐ Restrict your cookware to glass, stainless steel, or ceramic.

- ☐ Avoid buying aluminum pots and pans or nonstick cookware; if you have nonstick cookware, take good care of them so that they will last a long time.

- ☐ Do not use imported pottery with lead-based paint.

- ☐ Don't buy plastic or polystyrene foam drinking glasses.

- ☐ Do not store food in plastic containers.

- ☐ Check that counter surfaces are hard and smooth with well-sealed joints so moisture and food do not get trapped in the seams.

Major Appliances

- ☐ Always look for the Energy Star label when replacing appliances.

- ☐ Make sure your refrigerator is an energy-efficient model.

Energy Star®

Shoppers are increasingly seeing the Energy Star label on appliances and electronics, even on new homes. Energy Star represents a joint effort between the U.S. Environmental Protection Agency and the U.S. Department of Energy to endorse energy-efficient products and practices that can help consumers save money and protect the environment. In 2007, with the aid of Energy Star, Americans conserved enough energy to avoid greenhouse gas emissions equivalent to 27 million cars—while saving $16 billion on utility bills.

☐ Avoid continuous-cleaning ovens; if you have a self-cleaning model, don't run the cleaning cycle.

☐ Make sure your gas range has spark ignition, not a pilot light.

☐ If there is not a ventilation hood or exhaust fan over your stove, install one.

Bathroom

☐ Install a water-saving toilet.

☐ Shop for 100 percent organic cotton bath linens and a hemp shower curtain.

☐ Use a water-conserving showerhead.

☐ Check pipes for leaks to avoid mold and mildew.

☐ Lower the level of water fill in the toilet tank to conserve water.

Basement

☐ Check for dampness in wall or slab cracks, and make repairs accordingly.

☐ Ensure plumbing pipes do not leak or sweat.

☐ Replace any damp or hardened insulation.

☐ Make sure there are no musty odors or mildew stains on floors or walls.

Attic

- [ ] Install a whole-house fan in the attic to improve air circulation.

- [ ] Attend to any signs of moisture around the chimney, plumbing, vents, or skylights.

- [ ] Insulate your attic hatch.

- [ ] Make sure your attic air vent is not covered or obstructed.

Heating and Cooling Systems

- [ ] Regularly clean the filters in a forced-air heating system.

- [ ] Check any gas-fueled appliances annually for leaks.

- [ ] Make sure your chimney is sound, with no cracks.

- [ ] Ideally, the furnace and other utilities should be enclosed in a soundproof, airtight room to cut down on noise and air pollution.

- [ ] If paints or other flammables are stored in your basement, keep the area well ventilated, and make sure the lids are sealed to keep fumes from leaking.

Plumbing

- [ ] Avoid using polyvinyl chloride (PVC) or galvanized iron pipes.

- [ ] Check that there are no recently installed pipes with lead solder.

- [ ] Make sure your water has been tested for lead contamination.

- [ ] Have a professional check the floor drain for sewer gas entering the house.

☐ Make sure lights are placed at the front, side, and rear of the house for security.

☐ Check that any outside receptacles are protected with ground-fault circuit interrupters.

☐ Make sure that no heavy electrical wires cross the yard.

☐ Check that there is no treated lumber near the food gardens.

☐ Avoid using synthetic pesticides and herbicides.

☐ Do not mulch your garden with treated grass clippings.

GREENER GARDENS

☐ Plant trees to provide shade and wind protection for your house.

☐ Use plantings indigenous to your area.

☐ Opt for low-water landscape designs, such as xeriscape, and reduced water use by emphasizing native and/or drought-tolerant plants.

☐ Minimize high-maintenance landscaping with plantings such as turf grass.

☐ Install water-efficient systems in the garden, such as drip irrigation, which places the correct amount of water at the base of each plant, reducing waste from overwatering.

☐ Harvest rainwater for landscaping irrigation.

☐ Create an evaporative cooling pond in your courtyard or patio.

HOME RENOVATION

☐ Check out green building supply retailers, either locally or online.

☐ If you shop online, ask for samples so you know how the product looks and feels before you invest in any quantity.

☐ Install energy-efficient exterior lighting, such as high-pressure sodium lights that are appropriately sized for the location.

The Rural Builder

According to the Housing Assistance Council, development organizations in rural areas often have trouble finding green contractors or environmentally friendly materials. Despite of these difficulties, many rural groups are using the following strategies:

- Installing energy- and water-efficient practices including compact fluorescent lighting, Energy Star appliances, and low-flow water fixtures.

- Utilizing environmentally certified materials (e.g., certified wood products) and locally sourced materials.

- Effectively managing materials, resources, and waste, including use of recycled construction materials.

- Lessening site disturbance and erosion by using permeable paving materials

- Promoting resident training courses to raise awareness about living green.

Information on affordable green building in rural communities is available at www.ruralhome.org.

☐ Make sure flooring is formaldehyde-free and the wood is not from clear-cut forests.

☐ Purchase low-VOC paint.

☐ If you purchase bamboo flooring, make sure the wood is between four to six years old.

☐ Install a combined hydronic heating system, which uses hot water from the water heater for space heating.

☐ Consider using engineered lumber and wood alternatives, such as oriented strand board (OSB), as an alternative to plywood for sheathing, flooring, and roofing. Plywood typically uses old-growth wood, while OSB uses small pieces of wood.

☐ Use wood I-beams as an alternative to 2x6s or 2x8s for floor and roof joists. Wood I-beams use less wood to perform the same function and are often straighter.

☐ Consider laminated wood-fiber products, such as gluelam, parlam, microlam, etc., as alternatives to large-dimension lumber for trusses, beams, and headers, which use lumber from old-growth forests.

☐ Although it can be pricey, consider using certified wood for interiors. Certified wood is monitored by the Forest Stewardship Council (FSC) to make sure it is harvested, milled, and delivered under environmentally responsible conditions.

☐ Use composite lumber made from recycled plastic products as an alternative to wood for decking and fencing.

☐ Replace particleboard or medium density fiberboard (MDF) in cabinets and counters with form-aldehyde-free MDF alternatives, or products such as strawboard and wheatboard, made from agricultural waste.

Seal It Up!

Sealing particleboard with a flat, latex-based primer can prevent the outgassing of formaldehyde.

☐ Try fiber-cement siding as an alternative to redwood, cedar, or other types of siding. Fiber-cement siding does not rot or attract termites and is fire resistant.

☐ Install smoke and carbon monoxide detectors throughout your home. In some parts of the United States, radon detectors are also recommended.

☐ Install long-lasting, nontoxic ceramic tile in your kitchen and bathroom.

☐ Replace your vinyl flooring, which outgases VOCs and is petroleum-based, with linoleum made from renewable substances such as amber, chalk, cork, and jute.

☐ Consider recycled-content insulation made of fiberglass or blown cellulose. Blown cellulose (recycled newsprint) requires a special installer, but creates a tighter seal.

☐ Avoid treated wood that contains chromium or arsenic for decking.

☐ Look for decking materials with 50 percent or more recycled content.

☐ Consider Energy Star cool roofing products.

- [ ] Look for durable long-lasting roofing, such as metal roofing or asphalt composition shingles with a minimum 40-year guarantee.

- [ ] Choose durable windows and storm doors.

- [ ] Install vented rain screens between cladding and sheathing.

- [ ] Install flashing around windows and doors, and properly flash other water-entry points.

- [ ] Consider an HVAC system with carbon dioxide monitoring sensors.

During construction, make sure you:

- [ ] Protect trees and other natural features on-site.

- [ ] Use permeable pavers in asphalt or concrete to allow stormwater drainage.

- [ ] Connect roof drains to bioswales or drywells.

- [ ] Deconstruct existing structures in order to salvage reusable materials and fixtures.

- [ ] Save topsoil to reuse, or protect it from erosion during construction.

- [ ] Recycle 50 percent or more of job-site waste.

- [ ] Reuse form boards.

- [ ] Use recycled concrete for backfill or base under slabs and paving.

- [ ] Incorporate a minimum of 25-percent recycled fly ash in concrete.

REDUCING HAZARDS CHECKLIST

- [ ] Check all wood products before burning them or throwing them out. If the wood has been stained, painted, or chemically treated, don't burn it.

- [ ] Properly dispose of old cans of paint, varnish, stains, lacquers, turpentine, paint thinner, paint remover, and spray paint.

- [ ] Never leave paint- or thinner-soaked rags lying in your workshop. They are flammable and also emit toxins.

- [ ] Wear a mask and gloves when working with oil-based paints, stains, and solvents.

- [ ] Make sure there is a ground-fault circuit interrupter (GFCI) protecting each electrical outlet in your garage.

- [ ] Place a nonionizing smoke detector and a fire extinguisher in your garage.

- [ ] If you have an attached garage, make sure the separating wall is as vapor-proof as possible, and that there are no ducts or outlets that go from the garage to the house.

- ☐ Remove your screen saver, which is an energy waster.

- ☐ Turn off all peripherals when not in use.

- ☐ Unplug your computer when you are done for the day, or use a power strip to avoid vampire power leaks.

- ☐ Set your computer to go into sleep mode after a five-minute hiatus.

- ☐ Buy an ergonomic chair that promotes a natural spinal curve.

- ☐ Reuse file folders and mailing envelopes by placing a label over the old tab or address.

- ☐ Properly recycle photocopier toner and printer ink cartridges.

THE GREEN HOME OFFICE

- ☐ Replace some of your computer equipment with Energy Star models.

- ☐ Start using recycled computer paper or printing on the reverse for nonessential documents.

- ☐ Opt for direct deposit, online banking, and paperless statements to reduce paper usage.

Vampire Power

Even when they are turned off, appliances and electronic devices continue to use electricity. This sapping of current is called a phantom load, or vampire power. According to the U.S. Department of Energy, up to 75 percent of the electricity used to power appliances and electronics is consumed while they're turned off. According to the Ohio Consumers Council, this can cost homeowners an estimated $40 to $100 a year.

Rather than unplugging each device or appliance when it's not being used, switch to inexpensive power strips or surge protectors. Everything that's plugged into them can be turned off at once. By plugging your computer, fax machine, and printer into a power strip and turning it off when you're not using them, you can save roughly $6 a month.

On the Road

THE GREEN DRIVE

Follow these guidelines on improving your driving habits, fuel economy, and car maintenance—and you'll end up putting a green tiger in your tank!

☐ Get regular tune-ups and improve mileage by up to 4 percent.

☐ Check and replace clogged air filters to improve mileage by nearly 10 percent.

☐ Periodically have your car's emission-control system checked.

☐ Keep your car in tiptop repair; don't let odd noises or knocks go undiagnosed.

☐ Once a month check oil and fluid levels to keep your car purring.

☐ Change your oil every 3,000 miles.

☐ Follow the car manufacturer's instructions for the grade of oil you should use.

☐ Winterize your car in the fall to keep it performing at peak capacity.

☐ Always keep your tires properly inflated to get maximum fuel usage.

☐ Monitor your monthly fuel usage; if there's a sudden change in consumption, have the car checked by a mechanic.

☐ Get the junk out of your trunk to improve mileage. Every extra 100 pounds you carry around in your car reduces its gas mileage by one to two percent.

- [ ] Put in half a tank of gas at a time to reduce the weight your car is carrying.

- [ ] Use regular grade gasoline unless your car manual specifies premium.

- [ ] Patronize gas stations with vapor-recovery nozzles—the black, accordion-like devices attached to the nozzle.

- [ ] Never overfill your tank so that the gasoline spills out onto the ground.

- [ ] Use your car's GPS or an online map/locator to find the shortest route to your destination.

- [ ] Always listen to radio traffic reports before driving any distance to avoid areas of congestion.

- [ ] Avoid rapid "jackrabbit" acceleration when driving away from lights and stop signs.

- [ ] Coast your vehicle before you reach red lights or stop signs.

- [ ] Avoid aggressive driving, which not only reduces fuel consumption but also increases emission of pollutants.

- [ ] Follow the speed limit. Driving 75 along a 65 mile-per-hour stretch can lower your fuel economy by about 10 percent and release additional pollutants.

ELECTRONIC TOLL COLLECTION

Thirteen states and some municipalities offer electronic toll collection (ETC) systems. The most commonly known, E-ZPass, is found in Delaware, Illinois, Indiana, Maine, Maryland, New Hampshire, New Jersey, New York, Pennsylvania, Virginia, and West Virginia. Texas also offers ETC, with plans to make the North Texas Tollway all-electronic (with no cash option) in 2010. A 2005 study found that electronic toll collection systems reduce environmentally harmful emissions by up to 63 percent at toll plazas. With its relatively low deposit (for an ID tag), and beneficial discount plan, ETC pays for itself with regular use, as well as improves mileage by avoiding long, slow lines at the cash-only lanes. If electronic toll collection isn't offered in your area, next time you encounter the toll collector, buy a roll of tokens to speed future toll-booth visits (and avoid unnecessary idling).

- [ ] If it's available, participate in electronic toll collection or use tokens to avoid idling in the cash-only lane.

- [ ] Check to see if your company allows flextime—coming in and leaving work either earlier or later than normal—so you can avoid rush-hour congestion.

- [ ] Combine several errands into one trip.

- [ ] Don't drive long distances to a grocery store just to save a few dollars with coupons.

- [ ] While driving in warm weather, open windows or roof hatch to cool your car before turning on the air conditioning.

- Modern vehicles no longer need to warm up, so you don't have to sit for minutes with the car running.

- Modern cars also have automatic chokes, so you don't need to step on the gas pedal before starting the engine.

- In summer, find a shady parking place to keep your car cool and to reduce evaporation of fuel.

- If you have a garage, use it to keep your car warm in winter and cool in summer.

- Buy low-rolling-resistance (LRR) replacement tires that are specially designed to improve a vehicle's fuel economy.

- Keep your car's exterior clean to improve aerodynamics.

- Remove spoilers or whale tails that can create drag and affect mileage.

- Remove ski racks or bike racks during the seasons they're not in use.

- Avoid taking trips with a boxy luggage carrier on your roof. Try to fit your luggage inside the trunk or interior.

- When renting a car, try a hybrid or flex-fuel vehicle on for size.

- Consider using a gas-thrifty motor scooter for around-town errands or for commuting to work if you can avoid highway driving en route.

- When you're parking outdoors during warm weather, use a windshield shade in both the front and back windows to keep the car's interior from heating up.

NEW CARS

Traditional Cars

- Look for cars that can deliver 28 miles per gallon or better.

- Make sure you check the sticker for mileage ratings for both city and highway driving.

- Check emission levels online at the Vehicle Certification Authority Web site.

- Look for efficiency labels on the car. This practice will soon become compulsory and will extend to used cars.

- Consider a lighter-weight car. Generally, the lighter the car, the less carbon dioxide it produces.

- Stay away from cars with a whale tail or spoiler that creates additional drag.

- Avoid deluxe electronic packages that can increase fuel consumption.

The EPA's Green Vehicle Guide gives you information on the environmental performance of most makes of cars, vans, and small trucks. Log on to www.epa.gov/greenvehicles and type in the year and make of the vehicle that interests you. You can also do side-by-side comparisons of up to three vehicles.

HOW DO MILD HYBRIDS WORK?

Mild hybrids have traditional gas-burning engines, but they also feature an electric motor as a starter/generator and/or power booster. This means the engine is able to shut off when the car is stopped, braking, or coasting, then restart seamlessly when the driver accelerates. Mild hybrids are less expensive than hybrids, and many incorporate regenerative braking to recharge the battery. Mild hybrids can improve fuel efficiency by 10 to 15 percent. The mild hybrid also offers technologically cautious drivers a good stepping-stone to the full hybrid.

Hybrid Cars

☐ Rent a hybrid before you buy one to see how it fits with your lifestyle and sensibilities.

☐ Ask hybrid owners to talk about the pluses and minuses of their specific cars.

☐ Before you buy, factor in size, price, gas mileage, and appearance.

Typically, hybrids are $3,000 to $5,000 more expensive than their nonhybrid counterparts. But don't be put off initially by the higher price tags; prices will quickly start to go down as more people buy them, and there may be a tax credit you can get.

WHO'S MAKING HYBRIDS

Hybrids are currently manufactured by a number of major car makers, including Chevrolet, Ford, GMC, Honda, Lexus, Mazda, Mercury, Nissan, Saturn, and Toyota. They also come in a variety of styles, from sleek luxury cars and trendy SUVs to dependable economy cars. Soon pickups, minivans, and even sports cars will join the hybrid ranks.

Comparison Shopping

SURE, YOU WANT TO BE A GREEN CONSUMER, but how can you be certain that an item you're considering is earth-friendly? Before you buy, check this list for ways to determine if a product labeled "green" is truly green:

GREEN PRODUCTS

☐ Does the manufacturer provide a written, working environmental policy? Can you find it on their Web site or in their product literature?

☐ Does the manufacturer's policy strive to make improvements in manufacturing, reducing waste, and reusing first, then recycling?

Eco-Labels

An eco-label provides information about the environmental benefits of a product to consumers. In contrast to "green" symbols or claims made by manufacturers, an eco-label is awarded by an impartial third party that has independently determined that the product meets certain environmental criteria. Eco-labels differ from first party certification, where a manufacturer provides a label to promote its own products' environmental record, or second-party certifications, where a trade association verifies that a product meets certain criteria.

- [ ] Do they comply with their industry's voluntary testing programs?

- [ ] What raw materials are used to create the product?

- [ ] Where do these materials come from?

- [ ] Did the materials come from renewable resources?

- [ ] Are adhesives, coatings, or finishes needed?

- [ ] What are they made of?

- [ ] Is the manufacturing process energy efficient?

- [ ] Does the manufacturing process release harmful substances?

- [ ] Does the product ensure the health and well-being of the home's occupants?

- [ ] Does the product do the job well?

- [ ] How much energy does it use?

- [ ] Does the product release volatile organic compounds, and at what rate?

- [ ] How is the product packaged and transported?

- [ ] How is the product installed and maintained?

- [ ] Can safe cleaning products be used on the item?

- [ ] Is the product durable, biodegradable, or recyclable?

- [ ] Can individual parts of the item be separated for recycling?

- [ ] Can they be made into something else?

- [ ] Can the product be returned to the manufacturer at the end of its useful life?

- [ ] Is the price range of the product fairly competitive with nongreen products?

Source: www.regreenprogram.org

At Work

AT WORK

Whether you work in a big-city office or from your home in the country, whether you're the boss or a greenhorn, there are numerous things you can do to clean up your act. Saving energy and reducing waste will improve your mood and your bottom line.

Blu Horizons

Consider using Blu-ray discs at home and at work. Because they contain paper and can be shredded, they are easier to dispose of and recycle than normal CDs. Even though Blu-ray discs cost more, they have five times the storage of CDs or DVDs.

How Are You Powered?

Energy conservation practices can be easily put in place. Begin by looking at computer setups. Set machines to energy-saving settings. The easy-on/easy-off sleep mode will save energy during any absence, be it lunch, a meeting, or an offsite appointment. While screen savers may be pretty to look at, they don't save any energy. Also, if you plug printers and scanners into the same power strip with an on/off switch, everything can be turned off in one click.

☐ Whenever possible, store files on your computer or server instead of in traditional paper files. Back up your system every night before you leave.

- [ ] Keep your computer on its energy-saving setting and turn it off—or into sleep mode—at the end of the day.

- [ ] Remove energy-wasting screen savers.

- [ ] Shut off your computer if you're out of the office longer than overnight; it's good for a computer to get rebooted every week or so.

Lighting

Switch to compact fluorescent lights (CFLs). They come in myriad shapes and sizes. Though slightly more expensive than traditional bulbs, they pay for themselves after a few hundred hours of use, and last exponentially longer. These bulbs produce less heat in the workplace, thereby reducing cooling loads in warm weather.

- [ ] Go for lamps made of recycled glass, metal, or plastic.

- [ ] Install dimmers or motion sensors in conference rooms and bathrooms, places likely to go unused for extended periods.

- [ ] Consider a high-end LED desk lamp that uses tiny amounts of electricity.

Facts and Figures: Junk Mail

Junk mail doesn't only fill up your home mailbox—it can waste hours of the workday. For example, according to a report by the National Waste Prevention Coalition, the staff of a Seattle-area company's mailroom spent 25 percent of their time sorting through advertising-related mail.

What Are Your Printing Habits?

In the digital age, there are few reasons to keep paper files.

- [ ] Back up files electronically.

- [ ] File your e-mails away where they can be found readily and skip printing them out.

- [ ] Buy paper (and envelopes) with a high percentage of post-consumer recycled content and with minimum chlorine bleaching.

- [ ] Print on both sides of the page or use the scrap as notepaper.

- [ ] Recycle your printer cartridges with the manufacturer.

The Office Kitchen

Many offices have small kitchens with coffee machines, refrigerators, and microwaves. Bringing your own lunch in reusable containers reduces takeout waste. (It's also significantly cheaper and healthier.) If your office has a dishwasher, take advantage of it! Run a load every night or two so water isn't wasted by hand-washing.

☐ Bring your lunch to work in a reusable carry bag.

☐ If you're ordering takeout for lunch, ask around your office to increase the size of the order—and make the delivery more energy efficient.

☐ Implement a bring-your-own-mug policy, or ask your office manager to buy mugs, water glasses, utensils, and plates for office use.

☐ If your company or division doesn't have a water cooler, suggest that they install a water filtration system so that it's not necessary to buy bottled water.

☐ Keep a covered travel mug in the office for coffee and soft drinks. Take it with you to the cafeteria or lunch truck for refills.

☐ Save your chopsticks. If the takeout chopsticks you get are the nice, sturdy variety (not the

Working for the Green

If you're planning a job change, consider working for an eco-friendly company. Some firms actually give employees encouragement to go green, such as the Drive Green to Drive Change incentive offered by software giant Hyperion, whose employees get a $5,000 rebate for buying a hybrid car. Check out the career opportunities at Simply Hired's Eco-Friendly Companies search engine (www.simplyhired.com/ecofriendly) or SustainableBusiness.com's Green Dream Jobs section (www.sustainablebusiness.com/jobs).

splintery ones you have to break apart yourself that never separate cleanly), wash them and put them away in your kitchen or in your own desk drawer. (You can slip them into their paper packet to keep them clean.) This also helps you avoid having to use inferior chopsticks.

If you work at a large company, it may appear hard to do more than your own small part—turning off lights and biking to work, for example. You might be surprised, though, at how easy it is to convince management to make a few small changes.

The Infrastructure

Does your office need new furniture? If so, look into companies that use green, renewable earth-friendly materials.

☐ Go for wood and bamboo instead of plastic.

☐ Set desks close to windows to take advantage of natural light.

☐ Invest in lamps built with light emitting diodes (LEDs), a new energy-efficient technology that creates long-lasting bulbs.

☐ When it's time to upgrade office electronics, suggest Energy Star models to the purchasing department.

☐ Scatter a few green plants around your office or workspace to help filter allergens and pollutants.

☐ Make sure your workspace has task lighting, ergonomic furniture, and good air circulation.

☐ Buy green power. It costs slightly more to use renewable energy sources, but you'll be investing in a greener electric future.

Reusing & Recycling

Many companies are already on board, but make sure yours is up to speed.

☐ Make sure boxes are reused for shipments or recycled.

☐ Upgrading to a newer model? Donate your old monitor, keyboard, telephone, printer, or other electronic to a neighborhood non-profit or community library. At least make sure electronic parts are properly disposed of; many of them can be recycled, even the inscrutable circuitry.

☐ Start a recycling station for paper and cardboard; make sure to put one by the copier or main printer.

☐ Start a recycling station for aluminum cans and plastic bottles if one is not already in place.

- Reduce junk mail at work—which takes valuable time to sort—by requesting that companies remove you from their mailing lists. To remove old employees' names from lists, sign up at www.ecologicalmail.org.

- Cancel any trade journals or magazines that you don't read.

- Don't oversubscribe; order just one subscription to a trade journal, and route each issue through your division.

- Talk to the purchasing department about ordering recycled, low-chlorine bleached paper in general, and lower-grade paper for interoffice memos and notices.

- E-mail notices and reminders to coworkers.

- Send PDF files to anyone who needs to see a proof of a document before it goes out.

- Use misprinted pages as note paper.

- Use shredded waste paper as packing material.

Green Cleaning

Talk with your office manager about the office janitorial service. Do cleaners use nontoxic products? Are custodians trained in the safe handling of cleaners that contain chemicals? Is the plastic bag in your waste basket replaced every day—even when it contains only a few pencil shavings? See what products can be bought in bulk from earth-friendly companies. Ask the service to stock the bathrooms and kitchen with recycled paper products.

Green Commute

Get out of your car and onto the train. One person switching to public transit for their work commute can reduce daily carbon emissions by 20 pounds, adding up to 4,800 pounds per year. With the cost of gas and parking so high, perhaps it would even be less expensive to commute. (Buying a 10-trip or monthly pass will lower your per-trip cost and you won't have to pay the onboard surcharge.)

☐ Carpool. If public transit doesn't service the area of your workplace, try to carpool. Pedal or walk to a common meeting place (or drive to a stop-and-drive) and share the rest of the ride with coworkers.

☐ Telecommute if you can. Do you need to be on-site every day? Ask if you can telecommute one or two days per week. Some 44 million Americans telecommute.

☐ Arrange your schedule with colleagues so that each of you works four ten-hour days instead of five eight-hour ones.

☐ Ask for Transit Check. You'll save money on your commute by getting commuting funds pretax, and your employer will save money on payroll taxes—a win-win situation.

☐ Carpool to off-site events, meetings, retreats, parties, and luncheons.

☐ Share a ride to the airport with your coworkers for business trips.

☐ Listen to traffic reports before leaving for work so you can avoid areas of congestion.

☐ Measure the distance to work using various routes; then stick to the one with the least mileage.

☐ If you need your car for work, consider buying a hybrid.

☐ Suggest the next company car be a high-efficiency hybrid.

☐ Ride a motor scooter to work on clear days.

At School

SCHOOLS ARE GREAT PLACES to innovate and implement new environmental programs. Schools are the hearts of many communities, and can therefore gather and mobilize large numbers of people, including teachers, staff, students, parents, and concerned residents. Green projects can invigorate a school and benefit the entire community.

There are a number of ways to use the school lunch program to show you care about students' health and the environment.

☐ Visit a farm or neighborhood garden. Talk to farmers about their needs and how their production benefits the whole community. Combine this with lessons on nutrition and life cycles.

Facts and Figures

Despite all those stories about Grandpa "walking six miles to the one-room school house," these days just 31 percent of children who live a mile or less from school actually walk there. Only 2.5 percent of students who live within two miles of school bike there. Half of all students go to school by car instead of using energy-efficient school buses. The average mom with school-age children spends 66 minutes a day doing drop-offs and pickups, making five trips covering roughly 29 miles.

☐ Serve healthy snacks and meals made with food bought from local producers.

☐ Give waste from school lunches to farmers to use as fertilizers, or use it on the school garden.

☐ Plant a garden and raise your own crops. Ask a group of parents to oversee the operation. Create an after-school garden program in which kids work to grow their own food.

Food service isn't only about the food. Reduce food-related paper and packaging waste in the following ways:

☐ Use refillable condiment containers instead of individual packages.

☐ Dispense unbleached, recycled-paper napkins from health department–approved dispensers.

☐ Store produce and other goods in reusable containers.

☐ Work with vendors to reuse and recycle cartons food is delivered in.

Harmful products are too often used to control insects, rodents, and weeds. These toxins also leak into the ground and pollute the local water. Urge your school to switch from pesticides to integrated pest management (IPM). IPM is a common sense and low-cost practice that maintains a pest-free environment through safe methods.

☐ To keep pests outside, stop up all holes in foundations and walls.

☐ Empty out and clean lockers and desks at least once or twice per year.

☐ Wipe down all food-contaminated surfaces at the end of each day.

☐ Keep the school grounds clear of garbage. Ensure regular trash removal.

☐ Apply fertilizers throughout the year in small doses rather than one heavy application.

☐ Maintain at least one foot of space between outdoor plants and buildings.

Going Green at School

Institutions of learning, from grade schools to universities, are increasingly aware of the need to offer courses on environmental education. From elementary school fields trips to the local waste-transfer station to graduate courses on environmental engineering, the traditional "three Rs" of education have now been replaced with Recycle, Reclaim, Reuse.

Whether you are a teacher, a parent active in the PTA or PTO, or a concerned student, there are many things you can do to help your school become more green.

Below are some environmental improvement strategies you can suggest for your school. A school that addresses these areas can benefit by saving money through reducing consumption of goods and energy; increasing efficiency of operations and use of resources; creating more favorable learning and teaching conditions; generating community goodwill; avoiding future liability problems; and educating the next generation on the value of caring for the environment.

You can suggest improvements in:

- Energy use
- Solid-waste generation
- Recycling in offices and cafeteria
- Distribution of leftover food to food pantries
- Indoor air quality
- Pest management
- Mold growth
- Water consumption
- Athletic field management
- Laboratory waste
- Workshop waste
- Building renovation
- Purchasing

Source: Illinois Environmental Protection Agency, "Greening Schools," 2008

School Days

☐ Before your children start a new school year, sort through their old materials to see which of last year's supplies can be reused.

☐ Rather than buying plastic-coated textbook covers, make kraft paper or grocery bag covers, and let your children embellish them with ink stamping or stickers.

☐ Buy recycled school supplies, such as pencils made from old blue jeans and ring binders made from old shipping boxes.

☐ Use rechargeable batteries in mp3s, calculators, and other hand-held devices.

☐ Encourage your children to shop for school clothes in resale stores—tell them they're setting a new trend.

☐ Spend a little more on a sturdy backpack, so that your child can use it for years.

☐ Send your child off to school with a lunch packed in a reusable bag. Put drinks in a thermos instead of using disposable water or juice bottles.

☐ Remind your child to recycle in the cafeteria.

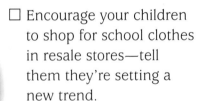

☐ Look for nontoxic craft products, glues, inks, and art supplies, such as water-based paints.

☐ Buy recycled computer paper.

☐ Avoid supplies with excess packaging, and buy pens and notebook paper in bulk.

☐ Save packaging, colored paper, egg cartons, and paper bags to use in crafts or scrap booking.

☐ Have your kids make locker decorations out of old CDs: add paint, stickers, glitter, rhinestones, pictures of pop or sports stars, and glue a magnetic strip to the back.

☐ Put a coffee mug on your child's desk to prevent the loss of pens, paper clips, and other small objects.

☐ Suggest that the school install a water-filtration system that would make bottled water unnecessary.

☐ Carpool with other parents to school, sporting events, and concerts.

☐ Encourage your child to walk home with friends several times a week.

☐ Look into renting decorating supplies for school dances, proms, and other events, and pass the information along to the school administration.

At School: College

Colleges and universities are self-contained communities that can act energetically and efficiently to address climate change. Higher education institutions are often excellent models for local governments and communities around the globe. As with businesses, colleges and universities should exercise conscientious control over their choice of vendors and products, from bricks to breakfast cereals.

☐ Encourage greener options. This includes purchasing green power. Because university buildings are powered 24 hours a day, investing in green alternatives can save the college money and prevent the unnecessary use of fossil fuels.

☐ Encourage student involvement. Get in on the act, starting with their home away from home, the dorm room. You don't need to start from scratch. National organizations, such as Energy Action's Campus Climate Challenge, are structured to involve students at universities across the country. Find a group that fits your college's interest and jump on board. Creating a national network builds momentum and increases effectiveness.

American College & University Presidents Climate Commitment

This nationwide group of more than 275 American colleges and universities has pledged to work independently toward making their operations carbon neutral. Urge your institution to join and learn from its peers.

Your Green Apartment

WHETHER YOU LIVE IN A SPACIOUS LOFT or a one-room studio, you can turn your rental into an earth-friendly space—and save money on wasted energy—by following these guidelines:

APARTMENTS

☐ Recycle all paper, glass, applicable plastic, and aluminum.

☐ Caulk any leaky windows, and place weather stripping along the bottom sills.

☐ Seal any air leaks around the air conditioner, and cover it with recycled plastic during cold weather.

☐ Change or clean the air-conditioner filter twice each summer.

☐ Use drapes to keep out strong sunlight in summer. Make sure the outer fabric reflects light.

☐ Install miniblinds that will keep out sunlight but still let a breeze pass through.

- [ ] Replace ceiling lights with compact fluorescent light bulbs.

- [ ] Place plants in draft-free areas of your apartment to purify the air.

- [ ] Don't store items in cardboard boxes, which can attract insects. Instead choose Tyga boxes, which are made of plastic that can be reused up to 500 times.

- [ ] If you have a thermostat, turn it down two degrees in winter and up one degree in summer.

- [ ] When it's time to replace major appliances, ask your landlord to install Energy Star models. Remind him or her that it will increase the value of the unit.

- [ ] Get permission to install an Energy Star ceiling fan to reduce the use of your air conditioner.

- [ ] If you have a choice about letting the exterminator in, politely decline, and look for natural pesticides in health-food stores or online.

- [ ] Place reflective foil behind radiators to maximize heat.

- [ ] Rather than cranking up the heat in the whole apartment, try an electric or hot oil radiator that can be moved from room to room.

- [ ] Plug multiple electronic devices into a power strip so they can all be turned off at once.

- [ ] Look for low volatile-organic-compound paints when it's time to spruce up the walls.

- [ ] Never use spray paint, varnish, or oil-based paint inside your apartment without wearing a mask and opening a window for ventilation.

If you're putting down carpeting, choose natural, untreated materials such as cotton, wool, or sisal.

If your apartment is on the small side, consider purchasing multifunctional furniture—sleeper couches, coffee or end tables that offer storage, or captain's beds with drawers underneath.

If the floors are uncarpeted, scatter wool or cotton area rugs around to act as insulation during cold weather.

If you're replacing kitchen or bath flooring, check out natural linoleum or unglazed tiles.

Develop a good working relationship with your landlord or management company so that when you need to bring up issues, such as a toilet that keeps running or drafts coming in under the door, you'll get a prompt, helpful response.

In the Bedroom

Use pillows stuffed with nonsynthetic filling or recycled polyester.

Consider buying a green mattress that incorporates natural latex foam or soy foam.

Shop for 100-percent organic cotton bed linens and comforter covers.

In the Bathroom

Install a low-flow showerhead and you will use up to 50 percent less water.

Lower the level of water needed in the toilet tank so that it takes less water to refill.

Put aerators on all your faucets to save water and lower water-heating costs.

Shop for 100-percent organic cotton bath linens.

Hang a hemp, soy, or bamboo fabric shower curtain.

Take shorter showers.

Use an indoor clothesline or laundry rack.

Replace the toilet seat with one made from bamboo.

In the Kitchen

☐ Opt for cookware in glass, stainless steel, or ceramic.

☐ When discarding old plastic glasses or mugs, replace with glass or ceramic.

☐ Prepare food with energy-saving microwave ovens, toaster ovens, crock pots, and rice cookers.

☐ Use green cleaners or a solution of white vinegar in kitchen and bath.

☐ Use a baking soda paste to clean ovens and greasy range tops.

☐ If your cabinets are composite wood, which outgas formaldehyde, ask your landlord if you can paint over them to seal in the fumes.

☐ Fill up your freezer because a packed freezer cools more efficiently.

☐ Shop for organic mop dish towels and flour sack towels.

GET YOUR ROOMS IN BLOOM

Plants naturally rid the air of pollutants and toxins. They also counteract outgassing and help balance the humidity in smaller spaces. By adding two or three plants to your living room, kitchen, and bedroom, you'll improve air quality and brighten your home. Most indoor plants don't need direct sunlight to thrive, because they originally grew in heavily shaded rain forests. The following plants are among the most effective in counteracting outgassing and balancing humidity:

- Areca palm
- Reed palm
- Dwarf date palm
- Boston fern
- Janet Craig dracaena
- English ivy
- Australian sword fern
- Peace lily
- Rubber plant
- Weeping fig

The City Lifestyle

☐ Walk or use mass transit whenever possible.

☐ If you rarely use your car, consider selling it. Rent one when you need a vehicle.

☐ Buy a bicycle and use it to run errands or to explore new neighborhoods.

☐ Ask friends or coworkers for the location of organic produce markets in your area.

☐ Shop the local flea markets and other venues for antique or secondhand treasures.

☐ Eliminate junk mail by signing up at www.catalogchoice.org or www.greendimes.com to be taken off mailing lists, and sign up at www.optoutprescreen.com to stop getting prescreened credit card offers.

☐ Cancel subscriptions to magazines you never read.

☐ Do all your banking and bill paying online to reduce paper overload.

☐ Save on the cost of books and magazines by joining your local library.

☐ Organize a neighborhood or block association or scout troop to clean up a vacant lot or a wooded lot in your town.

America's 20 Greenest Cities

If you're an apartment dweller on the move, you might want to choose you next city based on its green credentials. In 2008 *Popular Science* used data from the U.S. Census Bureau and the National Geographic Society's Green Guide to determine American's top 50 green cities. The results were based on ratings in more than 30 categories, including air quality, electricity use, green living, recycling, and transportation habits. Here are their top 20 choices:

1. Portland, Oregon
2. San Francisco, California
3. Boston, Massachusetts
4. Oakland, California
5. Eugene, Oregon
6. Cambridge, Massachusetts
7. Berkeley, California
8. Seattle, Washington
9. Chicago, Illinois
10. Austin, Texas
11. Minneapolis, Minnesota
12. St. Paul, Minnesota
13. Sunnyvale, California
14. Honolulu, Hawaii
15. Fort Worth, Texas
16. Albuquerque, New Mexico
17. Syracuse, New York
18. Huntsville, Alabama
19. Denver, Colorado
20. New York, New York

Portland, Oregon, aka "Rose City," gets half its power from renewable sources, and a quarter of the city's workforce commutes by bike, carpool, or public transportation. Portland also boasts 35 buildings certified by the U.S. Green Building Council.

- Go meatless at dinner or lunch once or twice a week.

- If you have a balcony or yard access, start a container garden with cherry or grape tomatoes and chili peppers.

- Put a small tree on your balcony to block the sunlight in summer.

- Grow aromatic herbs on your kitchen windowsill.

- Patronize restaurants that sell local produce or use eco-friendly carry-out containers.

- Don't patronize fast food restaurants that overpackage everything.

- Use recycled paper in your home office.

- Use phosphate-free detergents at the coin laundry or your building's laundry room.

- Twice a year, purge your closets and give away the clothing to a charity.

- Organize an apartment-wide sidewalk sale to get rid of unwanted household items.

Making a "Green" Move

Nothing reminds you of how much stuff you've accumulated as when you're packing up for a move. Here are some tips for paring down and keeping your move earth-friendly.

- Donate any clothing you no longer wear to a charitable organization.

- Sort through your possessions, and hold a yard sale to get rid of superfluous things.

- Before tossing out old electronics, visit www.mygreenelectronics.org to find an electronics recycler in your area.

- Books are very heavy to move; consider donating several boxes to your local library.

- Buy a limited amount of food the week before you move so that nothing goes to waste.

- Give any perishable items to a neighbor or donate canned goods to a shelter.

- Packing supplies such as foam peanuts and bubble wrap create lots of extra trash. Use blankets, linens, and towels as padding instead. Use recyclable newspaper as outer packing.

- When packing, consider using Tyga boxes, which are made of plastic that can be reused up to 500 times.

- Be aware that professional movers won't carry anything hazardous, such as items that are flammable, corrosive, or explosive (fertilizer, car batteries, liquid bleach, ammunition, and paint thinners).

- Once you arrive at your new home, investigate what recycling and waste services are available, and what the pickup schedule is.

- Make sure you recycle your cardboard boxes after the move.

recyclable

Afterword: Looking Forward

AS THE OWNER OF AN EARTH-FRIENDLY HOME, you'll probably be pleased to learn that the green movement has taken hold in the United States as well as in many parts of the globe. Although the concepts of sustainable living and carbon neutrality are gaining momentum, there are still plenty of roadblocks to truly sweeping change. People can be suspicious of new ideas and will often resist change, especially if it comes with the perception of "doing without," or "paying a price."

So what can you do to help things along? If you've applied the methods and suggestions presented in this book, you've already made a significant dent in your carbon footprint. You're conserving energy and water, recycling and reducing waste, and buying eco-friendly products. You're monitoring your car use and relying on mass transit whenever possible. But sometimes just setting a good example isn't enough. You've walked the walk, now maybe it's time to talk the talk—by encouraging others to go green.

SPREADING THE WORD

Your first step could be telling friends, coworkers, and family what you're doing and why. You don't need to preach to them, but simply point out how you are saving money on fuel and utility bills. Your words are bound to make an impression. If you've switched to a renewable energy source in your home or car, mention the tax breaks that

Good News on the Green Front

- In 2007 the House Education and Labor Committee passed the Green Jobs Act, which will prepare workers for "green collar" jobs, specifically those in the renewable energy and energy-efficiency industries. The $120 million in funding will establish state and national training programs and create an estimated 35,000 new jobs.

- Online auction sites, such as eBay and Goodwill (http://www.shopgoodwill.com/), not only keep tons of used, unwanted goods out of landfills, they also recently became the template for trade-in sites that eliminate the auction process and allow interested consumers to "buy it now."

- As increasing numbers of major petroleum companies face hefty fines and court cases over oil spills, illegal price hikes, and criminal disregard of the Clean Air Act, investors are increasingly channeling their money to green energy sources.

- Flipswap offers store credits or cash for used cell phones, which they then repurpose and give to the needy. In 2007, they recycled phones to the equivalent of 50 tons of solid waste. They also plant a tree for every phone swapped. Look for Flipswap at 4,000 participating retailers or online.

- In spite of the current U.S. housing slump, the green building industry posted revenues of more than $12 billion in 2007. This figure is expected to exceed $42 billion by 2015.

- Even toy makers are getting on the Green Wagon, manufacturing tea and dining sets and sandbox and garden toys by reprocessing plastic milk jugs into a safe, clean plastic called high-density polyethylene.

- Sustainable energy has become the watchword of many high-tech companies. Google's facility has gone solar, and a group of computer manufacturers are currently developing a climate-safe PC.

Future Innovations to Shrink Your Carbon Footprint

- While compact fluorescent bulbs are more energy efficient than standard incandescent bulbs, their benefits will soon be surpassed by light-emitting diode (LED) technology.

- Insulating double-glazed windows come standard on most new homes, but within three years transition metal switchable windows—which electronically create a mirrored effect to reflect heat away from the home—will become the model of choice.

- Within 10 years expanded-fiberglass insulation will give way to airtight vacuum-insulated panels, which use the same insulating principle as a Thermos bottle.

- Engineers are working on updating the water-conserving dual-flush toilet: developing an even more energy-efficient self-cleaning toilet.

- IBM is researching a new photovoltaic cell that focuses more sunlight into the chip to boost its power.

you're receiving from the government. Bring in some specimens from your organic garden or window box to show that practicing green gardening is healthier for both humans and wildlife. Give homemade organic treats, low-flow showerheads, organic cotton sheets, or carbon credits as gifts—and talk up the benefits. In lieu of gifts for yourself, ask people to donate to environmental organizations.

COMMUNITY CLEANUPS

Another step is getting together with other concerned individuals in your community to sponsor highway or stream cleanup or local "litterplucks." Work with your group to improve neighborhood recycling or to promote hazardous waste pickup. Have your group offer to organize a "green fair" at a local college campus, where green businesses can promote their services and discuss employment opportunities.

At work, make sure your company is recycling paper, cans, plastic, and glass. Encourage the

Adopt Endangered Animals

Most children love animals, and what better way to introduce them to earth-friendly issue than letting them adopt an individual from an endangered species. For example, for about $25, you can to "adopt" a sea otter through the World Wildlife Fund (WWF). The smallest marine mammal, otters love to spend hours in the water, and they are one of the few mammals that use tools. Now protected by law from hunters, the sea otter can use your help to stay protected. The WWF will send you an adoption certificate and a photo of the otter. Higher-premium membership plans include a plush stuffed animal and other goodies.

The otter isn't the only animal out there that needs your help either. Endangered or threatened species, such as the polar bear, panda, and penguin are just a few of the animals that are up for adoption through the WWF. You and your child can help the world's animals before it's too late, and adopt an otter or even an elephant.

cafeteria management to purchase locally grown produce, locally baked bread, and fair-trade coffee. Ask the company to reward carpoolers with small gifts or other incentives.

If you are highly ambitious and don't mind speaking in front of people, volunteer to give a talk to a local civic group about your decision to create a green home. Radio stations and local cable TV stations might also be interested in hearing your story—or you can offer to set up a panel discussion with green builders or green businesses in your area. Consider writing a column in a local paper or shopper on green options for homeowners. You might discover that many people would like to go green, but aren't sure where to start.

EDUCATING THE NEXT GENERATION

Perhaps the most valuable thing you can do is to make sure the children in your family understand the importance of conservation, recycling, and waste reduction. Many schools now include environmental studies as part of their curriculum, so offer to share what you have learned in your child's classroom or during an Earth Day assembly. By making children aware of the problems and offering them simple, kid-friendly solutions, you can begin a positive cycle that will have a lasting effect.

"We are made wise not by the recollection of our past, but by the responsibility for our future."

—George Bernard Shaw

However you choose to spread the word, you can be proud that you took a personal goal—making your home more earth-friendly—and used it as a platform to encourage and educate others. And just like ripples on a pond, your green consciousness will pass from person to person in an ever-widening circle.

Safe Deposit

IMAGINE LIVING CLOSE to a hazardous waste dump, with all its dangerous toxins and unhealthy emissions. Unfortunately, many people are not living near one, they are living with one. The average American homeowner has accumulated an estimated 100 pounds or more of potentially hazardous waste (aka HHW, household hazardous waste)—paints, finishes, solvents, cleaning products, pesticides, car and household batteries, gasoline or kerosene, and electronic devices. When these items have lost their usefulness, how does a conscientious homeowner dispose of them safely?

HOW TO DISPOSE OF TOXIC TRASH

Below are some guidelines for disposing of these products without creating a negative impact on the environment:

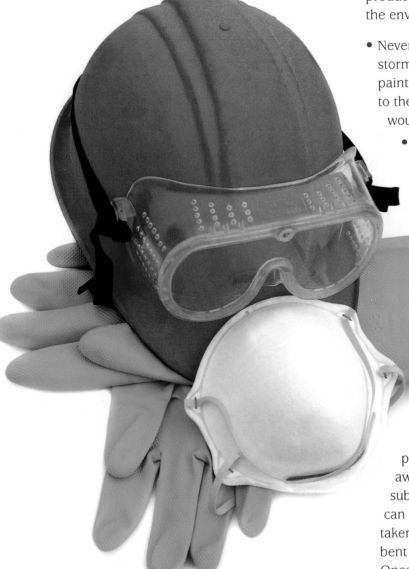

- Never pour toxic waste down the drain or into storm sewers. This includes motor oil, oil-based paint, varnish, and similar substance. Adhere to the rule of thumb: "Don't dump it if you wouldn't drink it."

- Never burn anything you think might be hazardous waste.

- Never store hazardous products in food containers. Keep them in their original containers with their original labels.

- The labels on some products contain instructions for safe disposal. A product can be considered toxic if the label cautions "wear goggles," "wear gloves," or "use in a ventilated area."

- Empty paint and varnish cans still give off dangerous emissions. Treat them as hazardous waste.

- Dispose of leftover latex-based paint by exposing it to air (in a safe place away from children and pets); if there is a substantial amount of paint left in the can, you can donate it (see the next item); if you get no takers for your old paint, you can pour an absorbent material, such as cat litter, into the can. Once the paint is absorbed, replace the lid and put the can in the garbage.

- Some waste disposal facilities offer exchange areas for unused or leftover paints, solvents, pesticides, and cleaning and automotive products so that they can be used by someone else rather than thrown away.

- Never bury unused chemicals or their containers.

- Antifreeze can be poured down the drain only if you are connected to a municipal sewer system.

- Do not use wood preservatives containing creosote, pentachlorophenol, or arsenic. Leftover wood preservatives, treated scrap wood, shavings, and sawdust should be delivered to a hazardous waste collection center.

Benefits of Proper HHW Management

- Reduction and recycling of HHW conserves resources and energy that would otherwise be expended in the production of more products.

- Reuse of hazardous household products can save money and reduce the need for generating hazardous substances.

- Proper disposal prevents pollution that could endanger human health and the environment.

Source: EPA, March 2008

- Certain products, such as smoke detectors, can be returned to the manufacturer.

- Many communities have a specific day for picking up hazardous waste. Check with your town clerk for the schedule. If your town does not offer this service, form a neighborhood committee to petition for hazardous waste collection.

- Many towns or counties now have drop-off facilities for hazardous waste, including electronic devices.

- Service stations will often take used motor oil and car batteries to recycle.

- Ultimately, the best way to reduce toxic waste in your home is to buy alternative, earth-friendly products whenever possible.

WHAT IS HAZARDOUS WASTE?

Broadly speaking, hazardous waste is any substance that might present a current—or future—threat to individuals, animals, plants, and the environment. Four criteria define a characteristic hazardous waste.

1. Ignitability
2. Corrosivity
3. Reactivity
4. Toxicity

In the United States, there are also four categories of listed wastes.

1. Nonspecific sources, such as a halogenated solvent

2. Specific sources, such as bottom sludge from wastewater treatment of wood-preserving processes using creosote and/or pentachlorphenol

TO AVOID CHEMICALS

The best way to rid your home of chemicals is to simply not bring them into your home in the first place. Here are some tips for toxin-free living.

- Buy nonaerosol sprays and biodegradable products that come in recyclable containers, and use the product only as directed and only when needed.

- Purchase rechargeable batteries. Nickel-cadmium batteries are more expensive than alkaline, but can be recharged up to 100 times. This saves money in the long run and helps to keep toxic metals out of the local landfill or incinerator.

- Buy multipurpose products. Look for nonphosphate, biodegradable laundry detergent that cleans and bleaches and an all-purpose household cleaner that can be used for a variety of washable surfaces: walls, tiles, floors, countertops, glass, ceramics, and wood. The product label should list the ingredients, instructions for use, storage, and disposal, potential hazards, and warnings.

- Compare a number of products; select the least toxic product; and buy only the amount needed.

Source: NOAA (National Oceanic and Atmospheric Administration), 2007

3. Commercial chemical products, inter-medi-
ates or off-specification products. There
are two lists for this category, one for acute
wastes and one for nonacute wastes. An
example of an acute waste is epinephrine. An
example of a nonacute waste is naphthalene.

4. Polychlorinated biphenyl. (PCBs)

Legally, any discarded solid or liquid that fits
into at least one of the following categories is
considered hazardous waste.

- It contains one or more of 39 carcinogenic,
mutagenic, or teratogenic compounds at levels
that exceed established limits, including many
solvents, pesticides, and paint strippers.

- It catches fire easily, such as gasoline, paints,
and solvents.

- It is reactive or unstable enough to explode
or release toxic fumes, including acids, bases,
ammonia, and chlorine bleach.

- It is capable of corroding metal containers,
such as tanks, drums, and barrels (such as
industrial cleaning agents and oven and drain
cleaners).

STORING HOUSEHOLD CHEMICALS

There is no avoiding the fact that there are
chemicals in and around your home, so storing
them properly is a consideration.

- Store products with lids tightly closed. Harmful
fumes may escape from an open container;
acid may splash the person who reaches for
the container.

- Store products in their original containers in a
safe well-ventilated place, out of direct sunlight, and in areas not subject to temperature
extremes. Always store chemical products out
of the reach of children and pets.

Resources: Where to Shop

This list of manufacturers and associations is meant to be a general guide to additional industry and product-related sources. It is not indented as a listing of products and manufacturers represented by the information and photographs in this book.

All Things Green

http://shop.allgreenthings.com/store/pc/home.asp
A member of 1 percent for the Planet, All Things Green donates 1 percent of its net profits to environmental causes. If you are changing to a greener lifestyle, this site with help you get there.

American Apparel

http://www.americanapparelstore.com
Popular clothing brand American Apparel offers some vintage items as well as a line of organic unisex tees, onesies, and undergarments from boxer briefs to thongs.

Aveda

http://www.aveda.com
Aveda was founded in 1978 with the goal of selling plant-based beauty products to the masses. Now one of the largest organic beauty companies in the county, Aveda uses responsible packaging and renewable energy to make and provide all their products.

Bamboo Outfitters

http://www.bamboooutfitters.com
Bamboo Outfitters provides many different eco-friendly products, as well as plenty of links to other green Web sites and reasons why bamboo is right for you and the environment.

Beth's Boutique Candles

http://www.bethsboutiquecandles.com
Beth's Boutique Candles sells a line of long-lasting, dye-free soy candles with cotton wicks that burn for up to 80 hours.

Birkenstock

http://www.birkenstockusa.com
For the past 40 years, Birkenstock shoes have been providing a green lifestyle to those who wear them. Made from cork and other natural resources, Birkenstocks have replaceable soles and utilize hand-stitching to ensure product quality.

Burt's Bees

http://www.burtsbees.com
Derived from beeswax and plant oils, this company's products are usually about 99 percent natural with no artificial preservatives and chemicals. Burt's Bees also relies on recycled and reusable packing.

Cali Bamboo

http://www.calibamboo.com
This company was started in 2004 after a surf trip around the world. Founders Jeff Goldberg and Tanner Haigwood wanted to create a business that would make a difference in the world. Besides providing the world with an outlet for bamboo, Cali Bamboo also helps keep the world a little cleaner.

Cosmetics Without Synthetics, Inc.

http://www.allnaturalcosmetics.com
http://www.earthsbeauty.com
Cosmetics Without Synthetics offers more than 500 products that are free of synthetic chemicals. It has a makeup line called Earth's Beauty, and it also carries natural skincare, haircare, bodycare, and household products.

The Cork Store

http://www.corkstore.com
Originally founded in Europe in 1855, Jelinek Cork

came to the United States in the 1950s. The Cork Store is dedicated to providing quality cork to the world while preserving the supply of cork trees.

Eco Smarte Pool

http://www.ecosmartepool.com
Using natural oxygen technology, Eco Smarte Pool water is a 100-percent chemical-free way to keep your swimming pool clean.

Eco Zen Boutique

http://ecozenboutique.com
Eco Zen Boutique provides shoppers with an assortment of hand-picked organic products.

Fabric and Art

http://www.fabricandart.com
Carrying only high-quality fabrics, Fabric and Art uses organic cotton, bamboo, and soy to make all its fabrics.

Gaiam

http://www.gaiam.com
Offering information, services, and goods— including fitness guides, yoga information, and an eco-home and outdoor store—Gaiam evinces a healthy, eco-friendly lifestyle.

gDiapers

http://www.gdiapers.com
gDiapers come complete with a washable outer lining called a "little 'g' pant" and a plastic-free diaper refill.

GladRags

http://www.gladrags.com
Founded in 1992, GladRags Menstrual Alternatives offers washable, reusable cotton pads as well as a variety of alternative feminine hygiene products.

Green Feet

http://www.greenfeet.com
Green Feet shows how to change your lifestyle over to an eco-friendly one. Plus, for eco-chic brides, there's even a gift registry.

Green Karat

http://www.greenkarat.com
Green Karat uses recycled gold to make all its rings and helps to educate its customers on the effects of gold mining and the benefits of purchasing earth-friendly jewelry.

Greenloop

http://www.thegreenloop.com
Greenloop provides a variety of organic clothing from what they refer to as "conscientious companies." The site provides green clothing for men and women, including shoes and accessories.

Green Sofas

http://www.greensofas.com
This company was the first to offer eco-friendly sofas (using nontoxic glues, cushions made from natural materials, and hardwood frames from responsibly managed forests) for less than $1,500.

Horizon Organic

http://www.horizonorganic.com
Horizon Organic is one of the leading companies in organic dairy production. Eighty percent of Horizon's milk comes from family farms, and the other 20 percent is from two company-owned farms in Maryland and Idaho.

Inmodern

http://www.inmodern.net
Inmodern offers eco-friendly furniture for moms, dads, tots, and teens in chic, modern designs.

Juice Beauty

http://juicebeauty.com

Using organic juice concentrates and other organic ingredients, Juice Beauty helps keep skin clean with ingredients free of exposure to pesticides. Besides being organic, all Juice Beauty products are 100 percent vegetarian, too.

Kushtush Organic Eco Sleep Shop

http://www.kushtush.com

Kushtush sells the Coyuchi brand of organic bedding. Coyuchi is one of the top brands in organic bedding using 100-percent organic cotton, which has been found to offer allergy relief.

Loop

http://www.looporganic.com

A provider of certified organic cotton bedding and towels, Loop offers products made without harsh chemicals, which guarantee softness and purity.

Manton Cork

http://mantoncork.com

A family-operated business, Manton Cork was founded in 1921 and is one of the largest importers of cork products in the country.

Naked Juice

http://www.nakedjuice.com

Dedicated to keeping their juices 100 percent juice and 100 percent natural, Naked Juice adds no sugar or preservatives.

Nimli

http://www.nimli.com

Nimli sells everything from clothes to jewelry to pet toys, all made of natural and organic materials. Its goal is to sell only products that do not harm the environment.

Odwalla

http://www.odwalla.com

Odwalla provides all-organic juices that nourish the whole body. It also uses green energy to make its products, and only 1 percent of the company's wastes go into landfills.

Patagonia

http://www.patagonia.com

A clothing company, Patagonia tries to use processes that are the least harmful to the environment. The company donates a portion of its proceeds to environmental organizations, makes its fleece out of recycled plastic, and works to preserve the environment.

Pet Smart

http://www.petsmart.com

Dedicated to keeping your pet happy and healthy, Pet Smart can provide you with information on how to reduce your pet's carbon paw print.

Philips

http://www.philips.com

Philips has plenty of energy-efficient products including the new EcoTV. The company is working constantly to create new energy-efficient products.

Pristine Planet

http://www.pristineplanet.com

With options that allow comparisons by brand and price, Pristine Planet sells everything from clothing to furniture.

Rowe Furniture

http://www.rowefurniture.com

With its new Eco-Rowe collection, Rowe Furniture now sells eco-friendly upholstery as well as sofas.

Satara

http://www.satara-inc.com
Satara provides earth-friendly clothes and products for baby and home alike, including baby carriers and bamboo bedding.

Seventh Generation

http://www.seventhgeneration.com
A producer, and distributor of earth-friendly household products, Seventh Generation makes cleaners, paper products, and personal care, including baby essentials and organic clothing. This socially conscious company also includes a Web log and tips for living the green life.

Silk

http://www.silksoymilk.com
Silk helps the lactose-challenged and saves the environment in the process. Silk is made using wind energy, preventing more than 16,000 tons of greenhouse gases.

Square One Organic Vodka

http://www.squareonevodka.com
Crafted from 100 percent organic American rye, Square One Vodka is made from ingredients so pure, the distillation process (to remove impurities) is shortened immensely. Even the label—made from bamboo, bagasse (sugar cane), and cotton— is natural.

Starbucks

http://www.starbucks.com
Starbucks is determined to help the environment throughout the entire coffee process, starting with the farmers and ending with the customers. By switching to recycled-paper sleeves and cups, Starbucks saves about 78,000 trees a year.

Smith & Fong

http://www.plyboo.com/index.php
Manufacturing a line of flooring known as PlyBoo, Smith & Fong offers a variety of bamboo flooring that mimics other woods, as well as other eco-friendly plywood products.

Stonyfield Farm

http://stonyfield.com
Stonyfield Farm has been using all-natural and organic ingredients for the past 25 years. Besides its ingredients, the company attempts to cut energy costs by using solar energy and donates 10 percent of its profits to earth protection efforts.

Trader Joe's

http://www.traderjoes.com
Trader Joe's has been providing high-quality organic produce since 1958.

Under the Nile

http://www.underthenile.com
Under the Nile uses organic cotton to make baby clothes, including organically friendly elements for buttons, such as wood or shell.

Whole Foods

http://www.wholefoodsmarket.com
With one of its core values being to sell the highest quality natural and organic foods, Whole Foods is one of the biggest chain suppliers of organic foods. It is also one of the most energy-efficient companies, using 100 percent green power for its power load, and has stopped offering plastic bags in all of its stores.

References

BOOKS

Attracting Birds, Butterflies and Other Backyard Wildlife
David Mizejewski

Projects to attract colorful butterflies, uplifting songbirds, and lively toads to a personal garden space, giving pleasure to nature lovers of all ages.

The Complete Guide to the Green Home: The Good Citizen's Guide to Earth-friendly Remodeling and Home Maintenance
Philip Schmidt

A great handbook for remodeling and repair projects that are environmentally sound. Projects include kitchen remodeling, flooring, lighting, and landscaping,

Easy Care Guide to Houseplants
Jack Kramer

Featuring more than 200 plants, this book explains the care and maintenance of houseplants as well as how to propagate them.

Easy Green Living: The Ultimate Guide to Simple, Eco-Friendly Choices for You and Your Home
Renée Loux

Raw-food chef and TV host Renée Loux offers recommendations include her "Green Thumb Guides" for choosing nontoxic, eco-smart, and human-friendly products.

50 Plus One Tips for Going Green
Alicia Marie Smith

This book explains what renewable and sustainable resources are all about, why recycling is crucial to the war on junk, and why building and remodeling green are so important.

Go Green: A Guide to Building an Earth-Friendly Community
Nancy H. Taylor

A great guide for beginners, this book offers wise tips and helpful suggestions for going green, such as upping fuel economy and green building techniques.

Go Green, Live Rich: 50 Simple Ways to Save the Earth (and Get Rich Trying)
David Bach

Internationally renowned financial expert and bestselling author David Bach outlines fifty ways to make your life, your home, your shopping, and your finances greener—and shows how your efforts can be financially rewarding.

Gorgeously Green: 8 Simple Steps to an Earth-Friendly Life
Sophie Uliano,
with a foreword by Julia Roberts

This eight-step program addresses life's daily challenges to a greener existence.

The Green Book: The Everyday Guide to Saving the Planet One Simple Step at a Time
Elizabeth Roger

This book is packed with simple tips and celebrity advice for preserving the earth's natural resources.

Green Chic: Saving the Earth in Style
Christie Matheson

Printed on recycled paper, and a portion of the proceeds going to charitable green causes, this cute and chic book is loaded with earth-saving tips that are stylish and fun.

The Green Guide: The Complete Reference for Consuming Wisely

The editors of *Green Guide* magazine; with a foreword by Meryl Streep

This book draws from more than ten years of both the online and print versions of *National Geographic*'s Green Guide newsletter.

Green Living: The E Magazine Handbook for Living Lightly on the Earth

E Magazine

A resource for both light and dark green advocates, this book provides the building blocks to help you make informed decisions that will help the planet.

Green Remodeling

John D. Wagner

Remodeling with nontoxic materials that reduces home energy use, saves water, and supports the environment through the use of responsibly manufactured products or those derived from sustainable natural resources. Printed on recycled paper.

Green Up Your Cleanup

Jill Potvin Schoff

Printed on 100% recycled paper, advice and recipes for how to eliminate chemical household cleaning agents from your life and replace them with natural solutions.

It's Easy Being Green: A Handbook for Earth-Friendly Living

Crissy Trask

A day-to-day guide with simple, practical suggestions that anyone can put into action, with more than 250 eco-friendly tips.

The Lazy Environmentalist: Your Guide to Easy, Stylish, Green Living

Josh Dorfman

Host of the eponymous Sirius Satellite radio show, Josh Dorfman shows how to conveniently green your lifestyle.

The Little Green Book: 365 Ways to Love the Planet

Joseph Provey

Printed on recycled paper, a book packed with a year's worth of short tips, tasks, and facts designed to lead any reader to a more healthy, environmentally friendly lifestyle.

Live an Eco-Friendly Life: Smart Ways to Get Green and Stay That

Natalia Marshall

This book is chock-full of tips on ways to sustain a greener lifestyle.

Living Green: A Practical Guide to Simple Sustainability

Greg Horn

Greg Horn explains the simple steps necessary to improve one's own health, as well as to live more sustainably.

Living Like Ed: A Guide to the Eco-Friendly Life

Ed Begley Jr.

A committed environmentalist for more than thirty years, actor Ed Begley Jr. shows how to go about life in a more environmentally friendly way.

Ready, Set, Green: Eight Weeks to Modern Eco-Living

Graham Hill and Meaghan O'Neill

From the eco-experts at treehugger.com, comes a do-it-yourself guide to living greener.

True Green @Work: 100 Ways You Can Make the Environment Your Business
Kim Mckay, Jenny Bonnin, with Tim Wallace

A do-it-yourself manual for the working world, *True Green @Work* explores ways to go green for businesses and workers in their day-to-day office existence.

Wake Up and Smell the Planet: The Non-Pompous, Non-Preachy Grist Guide to Greening Your Day
Grist Magazine

An offbeat, and sometimes irreverent, minute-by-minute guide to making more earth-friendly choices in our daily lives.

AGENCIES

Environmental Protection Agency (EPA)
http://www.epa.gov
This government agency provides a wealth of information, from gardening and recycling to hurricane preparedness. Interactive features include an online forum and a blog.

Energy Savers
http://www.energysavers.gov
This joint effort of the U.S. Department of Energy, the U.S. Environmental Protection Agency, and the U.S. Department of Housing and Urban Development is a federal agency collaboration to help improve the energy efficiency in your housing choices.

Energy Star
http://www.energystar.gov
A collaboration between the Environmental Protection Agency and the U.S. Department of Energy, Energy Star offers valuable advice on products, home improvement, commercial infrastructure, and building.

Partnership for Advancing Technology in Housing (PATH)
http://www.pathnet.org
Supported by the U.S. Department of Housing and Urban Development (HUD), PATHnet offers a wealth of tools and information to help you to integrate advanced housing technologies into projects.

U.S. Department of Energy (DOE)
http://www.doe.gov
The Department of Energy strives to promote American energy security through reliable, clean, and affordable energy and strengthen U.S. scientific discovery, economic competitiveness, and improving quality of life through innovations in science and technology.

SUGGESTED WEB SITES

Daily Fuel Economy Tip
http://www.dailyfueleconomytip.com
This blog offers a new tip for fuel economy every day, as well as an online forum.

Eco Geek
http://www.ecogeek.org
A Web site devoted to using science and new technology to improve environmental conditions, Eco Geek was started as a graduate-school project and offers up to ten new articles a day.

Green Options
http://GreenOptions.com
Launched in February of 2007, this site offers a community of environmentally mindful bloggers

that convey news and advice and facilitate discussion.

Grist Magazine

www.grist.org
An irreverent, no-punches-pulled look at environmental journalism, *Grist* comes complete with puns and jokes, blogs, and podcasts.

Responsible Shopper

http://www.coopamerica.org/programs/rs
A site that keeps track of which companies are environmentally sound—or not. You can search a company by name or its industry.

Treehugger

http://www.treehugger.com
A hipster-oriented site committed to being cutting-edge and informed, interacting with like-minded people in an online community, and taking action to help the planet.

GREEN ARCHITECTURE AND DESIGN

Kevin deFreitas Architects, AIA
Design + Build

885 Albion St.
San Diego, CA 92106
(619) 222-9831
http://www.defreitasarchitects.com
Kevin deFeistas Architects specialized in single-family custom residential and mixed-use urban development. The company's Casa Futura was named the Electronic Home's House of the Year for 2008.

Michelle Kaufmann Designs

580 Second St., Ste. 245
Oakland, CA 94607
(510) 271-8015
http://www.mkd-arc.com
This eco-friendly firm has designed several models of modular homes, including the Glidehouse™, mkLotus™, Sidebreeze, mkLoft™, mkSolaire™, and Sunset® Breezehouse™.

ONteriors™

16835 West Bernardo Dr., Ste. 100
San Diego, CA 92127
(858) 455-1234
http://onteriors.com
ONteriors designs and installs technology systems that enhance customer comfort and promote the development of environmentally responsible buildings and communities.

Organic Architect

615 Sansome St., Studio Three,
San Francisco, CA 94111
(415) 986-2728
http://www.organicarchitect.com
Architect, author, and educator Eric Corey Freed promotes both an organic and individual approach to design.

OTHER SERVICES

Infrared Diagnostic & Energy Audit
Flemming Lund, Certified in Building Science

9 Elaine Rd.
Sudbury, MA 01776
(508) 353-2381
http://infrareddiagnostic.com
Using infrared thermography and thermal imaging—combined with depressurization blower door, moisture meter and digital psychrometer—Infrared Diagnostic & Energy Audit uses the latest technology to provide clients with the most thorough building diagnostic reports.

Join Up

Appalachian Mountain Club

http://www.outdoors.org
Founded in 1876, the Appalachian Mountain Club promotes the protection of nature in the Northeast. AMC offers more than 8,000 trips each year and information on helping to keep the trails, mountains, and rivers of the Northwest in good shape.

Audubon Society

http://www.audubon.org
With chapters all over the world, Audubon (named after leading nineteenth-century naturalist and bird portraitist John James Audubon) hopes to conserve and restore the world's natural ecosystems. The organization works to achieve this goal through education programs, a magazine, and advocacy campaigns through its Web site.

Calvert Foundation

http://www.calvertfoundation.com
The Calvert Foundation is a nonprofit organization that provides investors with products and services that can help communities fight poverty and environmental issues. Impoverished communities are offered the money they need, when they need it, and where they need it the most.

John James Audubon (1785–1851)

Though John Audubon has no direct link to the society that bears his name, he was a talented wildlife artist in the nineteenth century. Most famous for his painting of American birds, Audubon's works are still popular today. Audubon's widow, Lucy, tutored one of the founders of the Audubon Society, George Bird Grinnell. When he founded an organization to protect birds and their natural habitats in the late 1800s, Grinnell used Audubon's name because of his legacy as a lover of wild birds and nature.

Clean Air Council

http://www.cleanair.org

A nonprofit environmental organization that fights air pollution, the Clean Air Council uses education and advocacy to enforce environmental laws.

ClimateCorps

http://www.climatecorps.org

ClimateCorps is an online encyclopedia that focuses on the impact of global warming. It also offers suggestions for stopping global warming and maintaining earth-friendly lifestyles.

Conservation International

http://www.conservation.org

Conservation International aims to demonstrate that society can coexist harmoniously with nature. Using a "Future for Life" strategy to bring together innovation, awareness, and effectiveness, this nonprofit hopes to saves species, conserve natural habitats, and give local communities the skills needed to achieve these goals.

Co-op America

http://www.coopamerica.org

Co-op America is an organization devoted to creating a sustainable society through education, community work, and the development of corporate responsibility in today's economy.

Earth Day Network (EDN)

http://www.earthday.net

This organization, founded by the organizers of Earth Day, promotes community awareness and the creation of positive change in how the environment is treated. EDN hopes to educate and encourages volunteers to be active in getting the word out about the troubles of global warming and the effect on the environment.

Earthjustice

http://www.earthjustice.org

Earthjustice is a nonprofit public interest law firm. It works for the environment in the courts and through Congress to get action taken to stop the progress of global warming and to preserve the planet's wildlife and natural resources.

Environmental Defense Fund (EDF)

http://www.edf.org

The Environmental Defense Fund uses smarts, business, partnerships, and legal knowledge to help preserve our environment and work on resolving our environmental issues.

Friends of the Earth

http://www.foe.org

Friends of the Earth is working to find an end to global warming and allow people to live in a healthier and safer environment. Their Web site provides information and up-to-date news on the environment.

Global Green USA

http://www.globalgreen.org

Global Green is committed to building a greener society and safe drinking water for everyone. Through education and action, Global Green is seeing its dream become a reality.

Greenpeace International

http://www.greenpeace.org

Founded in 1971, Greenpeace International works to save the planet against the threats of global warming and the destruction of the world's natural resources. Greenpeace allows its members to contribute in any way possible to the organization from blogging to Web designs.

The Izaak Walton League of America

http://www.iwla.org

Found in 1922, the Izaak Walton League of America is working to save the environment for future generations. They work through advocacy programs and education as well as internal conservation programs. The magazine *Outdoor America* is the membership magazine of the league, and it helps members fully understand what is going on in the world today.

National Wildlife Federation

http://www.nwf.org

The National Wildlife Federation wants to "inspire Americans to protect wildlife for our children's future." It works to achieve these goals through blogs and information on global warming and the effect it is having on the planet's animal population. It promotes government action to help save the planet.

The Nature Conservancy

http://www.nature.org

This organization—devoted to preserving the Earth and the plants, animals, and natural communities that inhabit it—offers tools and news to lessen your impact on the planet.

Natural Resources Defense Council Action Fund

http://www.nrdcactionfund.org

The NRDC Action Fund is a government organization that is trying to create community action in the world's fight for the environment. It campaigns for wildlife protection, as well as protection for the wildlands and oceans, and the prevention of global warming. Robert Redford, Billie Joe Armstrong of Green Day, and Leonardo DiCaprio are just some of the supporters of the Action Fund.

1% for the Planet

http://www.onepercentfortheplanet.com

This organization commits companies to pledge 1 percent of their annual sales to environmental groups around the world.

Rails-to-Trails

http://www.railtrails.org

Rails-to-Trails Conservancy (RTC) works to enrich U.S. communities and countryside by creating a nationwide network of public trails from former rail lines and connecting corridors.

Rock 'n Renew

http://www.rocknrenew.com

Rock 'n Renew is a nonprofit organization that uses musicians to reach out to today's society and create excitement about a greener lifestyle. Rock 'n Renew artists include Jody Porter of Fountains of Wayne, Art Alexakis of Everclear, and Debbie Harry of Blondie.

True Offsets

Rock 'n Renew has teamed up with environmental experts to launch a carbon offsetting project called True Offsets. It contributes funds toward global cooling and plants fast-growing trees every month to restore a damaged ecosystem in Hawaii. The movement has also moved to New York City and Los Angeles and may be national one day.

Sierra Club

http://www.sierraclub.org

Founded in 1892 by naturalist John Muir (the guy on the back of the California quarter), the Sierra Club boasts more than a million members.

Walkable Communities, Inc.

http://www.walkable.org

This nonprofit helps whole communities, or parts of communities (such as neighborhoods, business districts, parks, school districts, subdivisions), become more walkable and pedestrian friendly.

Wilderness Society

http://www.wilderness.org

Founded in 1935, the Wilderness Society works to protect natural sites in the United States for current and future generations.

Worldwatch Institute

http://www.worldwatch.org

Worldwatch Institute dedicates its time and energy to finding new ways to have a more sustainable world and working to maintain it.

World Wildlife Fund (WWF)

http://www.worldwildlife.org

The World Wildlife Fund works to protect the world's animal population through a healthy, safer environment. Participation in the organization includes adopting an animal, donations, writing letters to local senators, and getting the word out about the harmful effects of global warming and habitat destruction.

John Muir (1838–1914)

John Muir has been called "the father of our national parks" and was one of America's most active conservationists. He explored the Sierra Nevada and Alaska's glaciers and survived to write the tales. Muir provided much of the inspiration for Theodore Roosevelt's conservation programs like Yosemite National Park. Muir formed the Sierra Club in 1892 to help establish many national parks and wilderness preservations.

A Green Glossary

WITH NEW EXPERIENCES comes new vocabulary. This green glossary can help you make sense of—and become more comfortable with—"green speak," terminology associated with your more earth-friendly existence.

A

abaca. A species of banana plant with stems harvested for fiber and used in making clothing and textile goods; a sustainable alternative to cotton.

absorption. The process by which matter or energy is released from one source and gained by another.

advanced framing techniques. A methodology of construction designed to conserve construction materials by using alternate framing methods; also known as optimum value engineering (OVE).

aerobic compost. Composting with the use of oxygen; provides a quicker, but more labor intensive, method.

aerodynamic. The motion of air as it relates to a moving object.

aeroponics. The process of using air or mist as a replacement for soil for plant life development.

agriculture. The practice of growing and cultivating the land.

AHA (alpha hydroxy acid). A natural type of acid found in fruits, plants, and milk that reduces signs of aging by lessening the appearance of fine lines and wrinkles.

algaecides, alkalis, acids. Elements used in pool maintenance to kill algae, raise base ph level, and lower acid ph level; can also be particularly volatile when mixed with chlorine.

air barrier. A material installed around a house's frame to prevent or reduce the infiltration of air into an interior that may be too hot, cold, or moist for comfort.

air pollution. Contaminants or substances in the air that interfere with human health or produce harmful environmental effects.

air sealing. The sealing of cracks and holes in a home's envelope to prevent uncontrolled movement of air.

annual. A flowering plant that blooms and expires in one growing season.

annual consumption. The amount of electricity used by a consumer in one year measured in kilowatt-hours (kwh). This information can be acquired from the electricity bill or energy provider.

B

bamboo. A fast-growing reed deemed an environmentally sustainable alternative to conventionally grown wood.

bat guano. An organic fertilizer that contains nitrogen, phosphorus, and potassium and is also a natural nematocide and fungicide.

beeswax. Natural wax produced in the hives of honeybees; a common ingredient in such things as candles, cosmetics, and pharmaceuticals.

biennial. A flowering plant that sprouts but does not bloom its first year, and blossoms the following season. Once bloomed, it expires. examples include foxgloves and hollyhocks.

biodegradable. A product able to be broken down into smaller organic materials by the natural action of living microorganisms.

biodynamic agriculture. An organic approach to farming that seeks to reduce the amount of strain and damage that comes along with overproduction.

biodiesel. A domestic, renewable fuel derived from natural oils, such as soybean oil.

biodiversity. The variety and range of living things that exist in the world, or a particular place.

biosphere. The atmosphere of the earth that contains all living organisms.

borate. A wood preservative that is nontoxic to humans, but is highly toxic to wood-boring insects, such as termites.

box schemes. A system in which boxes of locally grown or organic food and produce are delivered to people's homes.

C

cap and trade. A method for controlling pollution by providing economic benefits to companies or organizations that meet specific reductions in emissions. A government agency sets a limit on the amount of emissions a company may emit; different companies are given the right to emit certain amounts. Those who go beyond their cap must purchase more credits; essentially, purchasing these credits is the equivalent of being fined for pollution.

carcinogen. Cancer-causing agent.

carbon dioxide. A heavy gas chemical compound and greenhouse gas, warming the earth's atmosphere and propelling the greenhouse effect. Also known as CO_2.

carbon footprint. The total amount of greenhouse gases produced directly and indirectly to support human activity.

carbon monoxide. A colorless, odorless, and highly toxic gas often created during combustion.

carbon neutral. Describes a means of counteracting the amount of climate-damaging carbon emissions and eliminating them where possible.

carbon offsets. Funding projects that reduce the emissions of carbon, such as paying to plant new trees or investing in green technologies, such as solar and wind power.

cardboard mulching. Weed control used in sustainable agriculture; covering plants with layers of recycled cardboard and additional organic material prevents many weeds from crowding the plant.

carpool. A group of individuals that meets in one common area (or its members are picked up en route) to share an automobile ride to a predetermined mutual destination.

cellulose. A structural component of plants used to make biofuels such as ethanol and biodiesel.

CFL (compact fluorescent lamps). Bulbs that produce less heat and use reduced electricity; more energy-efficient than traditional lightbulbs.

chlorine. A chemical element and powerful oxidant used in disinfectants and bleaching. It is often used as a cleansing product in swimming pools. When freed from chemical bonds, it becomes a toxic gas.

chlorofluorocarbons (CFCs). Artificially created chemical compounds containing carbon, chlorine, fluorine, and sometimes hydrogen. Used to facilitate cooling in refrigerators and air conditioners; they deplete the ozone layer.

climate change. A change in temperature and weather patterns due to human activities such as burning fossil fuels.

clean computing. An organization's manufacture, use, and disposal of IT equipment that does not produce any harmful waste at any stage. Nonhazardous materials are used in microchip construction and packaging.

cob houses. Durable structures made of claylike lumps of soil, sand, and straw that can withstand long periods of rain without deteriorating.

compost tea. A "tea" brewed using compost and water and then applied to garden plants' leaves and base to prevent disease.

composting. A mixture consisting of various forms of decaying matter used for fertilizing soil.

composting toilet. Composting toilets come in several different types. They do not use water to flush away waste, but instead rely on aerobic bacteria and fungi to break down human waste. Also called dry toilets, biological toilets, and waterless toilets.

compressed-earth block (CEB). Construction blocks made with clay, sand, and a stabilizing ingredient like lime or Portland cement.

condensation resistance factor. A measure of the effectiveness of a window or glazing system to decrease impending condensation. The higher the condensation resistance factor, the more efficient the window system.

conflict-free diamonds. High-quality natural diamonds guaranteed as obtained without the use of violence, human rights abuses, child labor, or environmental destruction. Only ethical practices have been used in their mining, cutting, and polishing.

cork. Provides natural, thermal insulation, thereby helping to lower energy consumption, as well as absorbing sound and shock. Cork is harvested by peeling away the bark from the trunk and branches of the cork tree (*Quercus suber*) every 9 to 12 years and does not necessitate the felling of the tree.

CWMP (Construction Waste Management Plan). Diverts construction debris from landfills to be recycled, salvaged, and reused.

D

deciduous trees. Trees that shed their leaves during the cold or dry season, depending on the climate, and remain bare until new leaves grow in the spring; often referred to as hardwoods.

deconstruction. The careful disassembly of the building into its component parts, which allows many of those parts to be reused or recycled.

desertification. Land degradation in arid, semi-arid, and dry sub-humid areas of the world caused by a combination of factors including climate change and human activities.

DEET. A chemical pesticide and active ingredient in insect repellent.

DIY (Do-It-Yourself). As the name implies, DIY is a self-reliant way to create items and craft good without buying them ready-made.

dual-flush toilet. A water-conserving toilet that gives users a choice of low flush (using as little as 0.8 gallon) or a more powerful flush (which uses about 1.8 gallons).

E

earthen flooring. Earth compacted with straw or other fibers and conditioned with various oils to form a hard surface. Although labor intensive, these floors are easy to repair, and production energy is low due to the inexpensive materials.

earth shelter. A house that lies mostly beneath the ground surface. The surrounding soil provides natural insulation, making the house inexpensive to heat and cool. The best location for earth-sheltered houses is a well-drained hillside where windows face the south or an overhead skylight can fill the interior with sunshine.

eco-assessment. An evaluation of a home or workplace with the aim of cutting energy and water usage.

eco-bag. An ethically, organically made bag to use regularly for shopping instead of plastic or paper shopping bags.

eco-bus. A bus that uses any combination of bio-diesel, hydrogen, natural gas, and electric power.

eco-spun. A high-quality polyester fiber made from 100-percent certified recycled PET (soda/pop) bottles, and is capable of keeping about three billion plastic PET bottles out of the world's land-fills each year.

ecosystem. A community of plants, animals, and microorganisms in a specific environment functioning together as a unit.

ecube. A small wax cube placed in the refrigerator that mimics food; the cube is connected to the fridge's cooling system, which will respond to the wax's coldness rather than the air's temperature to conserve energy.

energy efficiency. Using less energy to accomplish the same task, which reduces air pollution and lowers costs; examples of home energy efficiency are weather stripping, a water heater blanket, and compact fluorescent light bulbs. When shopping for household appliances, look for the Energy Star logo to find appliances that use less energy and lower electricity costs.

electromagnetic field emissions. The production of electrons exerted from magnetic and electric fields, resulting in emitted electromagnetic radiation.

emissions (car gas). Gases released into the atmosphere as a result of fuel combustion.

emissions cap. A limit placed on companies regarding the amount of greenhouse gases they can emit.

energy sensors. A device that receives signals from heat, pressure, light, or motion and responds accordingly.

Energy Star rating. EPA's labeling program designed to classify and promote energy-efficient products to reduce greenhouse gas emissions.

engineered lumber. Design to reduce the amount of material needed for framing a building, requiring fewer trees and smaller dimension lumber that can be assembled in various configurations to span long distances with equal or superior strength.

Environmental Protection Agency (EPA). Governmental organization with the mission to protect human health and the environment.

ethanol. An alternative automotive fuel produced from grain and corn.

F

fair trade. Describes a sustainable system that empowers disadvantaged producers through payment of a fair price, thereby creating sustainable economies and new markets in otherwise poor developing countries.

farmers' markets. An association of farmers who come together on a regular basis to sell local food and homegrown produce.

fish emulsion. Nitrogen-rich fertilizer made from fish byproducts that were rescued from fish processing operations.

flat-pack. Furniture designed to pack flat. Flat-packing reduces shipping costs and the amount of fuel used in transportation.

flexible-fuel vehicle (FFV). A car with a single fuel tank, fuel system, and engine that is designed to run on almost all blends of gasoline and ethanol.

flow reducer. A device attached either just downstream from the water shutoff valve to a building or at the outlet of a fixture; designed to reduce the amount of water flow in relation to the delivery pressure from the street.

food cooperative. Community organization that purchases high-quality grocery items in bulk from worker- or customer-owned businesses, thereby reducing food costs.

fossil fuel. Hydrocarbons found within the top layer of the earth's crust.

fuel cell. A device, often powered by natural gas or electricity, that uses an electrochemical process to convert energy into electrical power, is cleaner than grid-connected power sources, and produces hot water as a byproduct.

fuel efficiency. The measure of how much functional energy is produced from a certain amount of fuel.

fungicide. A killer or inhibitor of fungus; can be chemical or natural.

G

geothermal. Heat produced from within the earth, used as a renewable energy source to heat buildings or generate electricity.

global. Pertaining to all-inclusiveness as in the context of worldwide, or involving the entire world.

green design. Resource-efficient and environmentally sound architectural design; its elements include solar panels, natural lighting, and sustainable construction materials.

green certificates. Documentation representing environmental attributes of power produced from renewable resources, resulting in clean power generators able to sell electricity to power providers at competitive market value. Any additional profit of the sale of the green certificates covers the above-market costs associated with producing power made from renewable energy sources.

Green-e logo. A certification mark registered and owned by the Center for Resource Solutions. The logo represents an electric power product conforming with and used in conformance with the requirements of the Green-e Code of Conduct. The logo may also be used by companies that have purchased minimum quantities of Green-e Certified Renewable Energy and have signed the Green-e logo use agreement.

greenhouse gases. Gases emitted into the atmosphere that diminish heat loss into space and cause global warming and the greenhouse effect. Water vapor, carbon dioxide, methane, nitrous oxide, ozone, and CFCs are all greenhouse gases.

greenhouse effect. The earth's atmosphere traps solar radiation, which produces atmospheric gases and warms the planet's surface, much the way a greenhouse traps heat.

Green Seal. A widely recognized green product certification. The Green Seal promotes products and services that cause less toxic waste, conserve resources, and minimize global warming and ozone depletion.

greenwashing. A marketing technique used by corporations who want to look more environmentally friendly than they really are.

H–I

heat-island effect. The increase of temperature in a city when natural landscaping is replaced with streets, buildings, and other infrastructures. This increase sparks the need for cooling energy, intensifies pollution, and contributes to global warming.

heat pump. A mechanical device used for heating and cooling that operates by pumping heat from a cooler to a warmer location. Heat pumps can draw heat from a number of sources, such as air, water, or earth.

heater efficiency. The energy efficiency of a heating mechanism is measured by its energy factor; the number shown on the EnergyGuide label, which incorporates the overall operating costs, efficiencies, and heat losses.

heirloom seeds. Seeds that have traditionally been saved by families, generation after generation.

hemp. An environmentally friendly fiber that requires no pesticides, herbicides, or fertilizers, and uses very little water.

herbicides. An agent used to destroy or inhibit plant growth.

HEV (hybrid electric vehicle). A car with both a battery and electric motor in its internal combustion engine, offering the extended range and rapid refueling of a conventional vehicle but with the potential for much higher fuel economy.

HDPE (high density polyethylene). Type-2 plastic; used for milk and water jugs, bleaches, detergents, and some body products.

household hazardous waste (HHW). Any substance that presents a current—or future—threat to individuals, animals, plants, and the environment; includes carcinogens, highly flammable materials, and any substance that corrodes metal or emits toxic fumes.

hybrid system. A renewable energy system with two different technological components resulting in the same kind of energy; for example, a wind turbine and a solar photovoltaic array combine as a source of power.

hydroelectricity. Renewable energy produced from moving water; it produces no waste and no carbon dioxide.

hydroponics. The use of liquid as a replacement for or in addition to soil for growing certain kinds of vegetation favorable to that particular environment.

invasive plant. A nonnative plant aggressively growing outside of its natural environment in a way that may be detrimental to the native plants, insects, and animals surrounding it.

K–L

kapok. A tree that produces a fluffy fiber in its seedpods. The kapok fiber is a substitute for down.

kelp. A sea plant used as an organic fertilizer.

leaking electricity. The power needed for electrical equipment to remain ready for use while in a dormant mode. Electricity is still used by many electrical devices, such as TVs, stereos, and computers, even when you think they are turned off.

LED (light emitting diodes). A device containing chemical compounds that light up when in contact with electricity. LEDs don't require a heating filament, so they burn cooler and use less electricity to produce light. They also last longer than incandescent and fluorescent bulbs.

LDPE (low-density polyethylene). Type-4 plastic used in most grocery store bags, most plastic wrap, and some bottles.

life-cycle analysis. The process of tracing a product, material, or practice from its origin through its final disposal or reuse for the purpose of tracking its energy efficiency.

light output. The perceived power of light, measured in the unit of lumen (lm).

losses (energy). A term applied to energy converted to a form that cannot be used effectively during the operation of energy production.

low-E (emissivity) glass. Infrared- and ultraviolet ray–blocking, energy-efficient glass that is coated with a transparent metallic oxide that limits solar heat gain.

low flow. Describes plumbing fixtures, such as faucets, toilets, and showerheads, that reduce water use by intensifying but decreasing volume of the flow.

M

marmoleum. A natural linoleum produced from renewable materials, including linseed oil, rosins, wood flour, jute, limestone, and ecologically responsible pigments. The harvesting and extracting of these materials consumes relatively little energy.

methanol. A clear, lightweight liquid that is used mainly as a fuel preservative. It is also known as wood alcohol.

microbrewery. A small brewery, producing fewer than 10,000 barrels of beer and ale a year and selling its products on the premises.

micro-irrigation. An irrigation system with small sprinklers and microjets or drippers designed to apply small volumes of water.

MPG (miles per gallon). The amount of gas utilized for every mile driven in a vehicle.

mulch. A ground covering placed around plants to prevent the growth of weeds, reduce soil erosion and water loss, and provide nutrients.

N

natural latex. Produced from white sap of rubber trees, this rubber-like substance is biodegradable and has a life expectancy of 20 years or more.

neem oil. Oil from Neem trees effective in houseplant pest management and leaf polishing.

nematode. Worms with unsegmented cylindrical bodies; some varieties are garden pests while others (known as beneficial nematodes) eat invasive insects including a variety of beetles, borers, crickets, flies, moths, and weevils; also known as roundworms.

nematocide. Substance that kills the wormlike creatures known as nematodes through natural or chemical methods.

NGV (natural gas vehicle). A passenger car that run on compressed natural gas (CNG), which emits less air pollution and carbon dioxide than gasoline-running vehicles.

nonrenewable fuels. Fuels that cannot be easily made or renewed, such as oil, natural gas, and coal; also known as fossil fuels.

O

off-grid. Living in a self-sufficient way without relying on public utilities.

organic agriculture. A method of farming that relies on natural forms of fertilizer and pest control rather than synthetic chemicals.

organic cotton. Cotton grown without pesticides or fertilizers and usually woven into textiles like bedding and towels.

organic wine. Wine produced from organic grapes (grown without chemical killers of insects and weeds, and without chemical fertilizers or fungicides).

organic wool. Wool produced from sheep that are fed organic feed and are not "dipped" to control parasites.

P–Q

paper battery. A flexible, ultrathin energy storage and production device formed by combining carbon nanotubes with a conventional sheet of cellulose-based paper that is nontoxic and biodegradable.

pescatarian. A person whose diet excludes meat, but who consumes fish, eggs, and dairy products.

PET (polyethylene terephthalate ethylene). Type-1 plastic used for most sodas, water, juices, detergents, cleansers, and some peanut butter jars.

photocell unit. Detects and monitors natural light values; at dusk the unit expels light, and at dawn it diminishes light. These techniques conserve excess energy.

photovoltaic panels. Solar panels that convert sunlight into electricity; power is produced when sunlight strikes the semiconductor material and creates an electrical current.

perennial. A flowering plant that lives for three or more seasons.

pesticides. An agent used to destroy insects that often cause harmful environmental effects.

post-consumer waste. Raw materials that were used by consumers, recycled, and morphed into something else.

PP (polypropylene). Type-5 plastic used in most opaque/clouded plastic food storage, syrup and yogurt containers, straws, and some baby bottles.

PS (polystyrene). Type-6 plastic used in poly-styrene foam trays and egg cartons, disposable cups and bowls, carryout containers, and opaque plastic cutlery.

PVC or V (polyvinyl chloride). Type-3 plastic used for cling film, some plastic squeeze bottles, cooking oil, and some detergent and window-cleaning preparations.

R

rapidly renewable. Materials that replenish faster than hardwoods such as bamboo and cork.

recyclable. Refers to products as paper, glass, plastic, used oil, and metals that can be repro-cessed instead of being disposed of as waste.

reforestation. Replanting trees to restore forest that has been depleted by overharvesting, disease, or desertification.

renewable energy. Energy derived from regenera-tive resources that cannot be depleted. Examples are moving water, thermal gradients in ocean water, biomass, geothermal energy, solar energy, and wind energy.

ROI (Return on Investment). A performance measure used to evaluate the efficiency of an investment or to compare the efficiency of a num-ber of different investments. For example, many "green" purchases can pay for themselves with long-term increased energy efficiency.

roof pond. A solar energy collection device using containers of water located on a roof to absorb solar energy during the day so that its heat can be used at night.

S

shading coefficient. The ratio of solar heat trans-ferred through a glazing material relative to the solar heat transferred through $1/8$-inch clear glass. Low numbers reflect minimal solar heat gain.

silent vampire. Any electronic device that still draws power from an outlet through a charger, even when the device is turned off, or it is disconnected.

slow food. A movement that emphasizes the local and regional production of food, especially focusing on the many traditions of food present throughout the world.

slush pile. A mound of mixed snow, ice, and ice water placed outside of a data center and pulled through a filter used to cool IT equipment, effec-tively reducing cooling costs.

soil conservation. The practices of planting and organizing a garden to reduce soil erosion. Methods include cover crops, crop rotation, and planting perennials.

solar charge. Energy generated from solar panels.

solar energy. Energy from the sun in the form of heat or light.

solar heat gain coefficient (SHGC). The percentage of heat gained from both direct sunlight and absorbed heat. Small numbers reflect the ability to reduce solar heat gain.

solar panels. A battery of cells that collect and covert sunlight into a useable source of electric energy.

solar thermal systems. Systems that collect and absorb solar energy for useful purposes such as water heating, space heating, and cooling.

solar water heating. Heating domestic water by allowing ground- or rooftop-mounted panels to collect solar rays as the water flows slowly through a series of small tubes. The heat transfer is then stored either in a potable drinking-water vessel (your water heater) or introduced into a closed-loop transport system to provide environmental space heating.

solar window screens. A mesh screen that is used to block insects as well as light and heat from the sun.

sustainable. Complying with the needs of the present without damaging the resources of future generations; a sustainable process can be carried out over and over without negative environmental effects or impossibly high costs.

sustainable forestry. The practice of managing forest resources to meet the long-term product needs of humans while maintaining forested landscape biodiversity with a goal to restore, enhance, and sustain a full range of economic, social, and ecological values.

T

telecommute. To work at home by the use of an electronic linkup with a central office.

thermal envelope. The thermal enclosure created by the building exterior and insulation. Improving the thermal envelope is a key aspect of creating an energy-efficient home.

thermostat. A device that regulates the temperature of a particular system by controlling the movement of heat energy.

tidal power. Power obtained by catching the energy of moving water masses due to tides.

transformer. A mechanism that changes one form of electricity into another by fluctuating its current or voltage.

tree-free papers. Paper made from roasted java, bananas, cotton rags, denim scraps, agricultural fibers, hemp, or flax.

U–V

U-value (U factor). A measure (often used for windows) of thermal conductivity that is the inverse of R-value. A lower U-value means a more energy-efficient window.

ultraviolet light (UL). Electromagnetic radiation with shorter light rays than visible light, most commonly found in solar energy.

vegan. A vegetarian who eats plant products only, excluding all derived from animals such as eggs and dairy.

vegetable- or soy-based inks. The use of vegetable oil as the vehicle for carrying pigment, as opposed to petroleum solvents.

vegetarian. A person whose diet consists mainly of vegetables and plants but does consume animal-derived products such as diary.

vegetated roof. A roof covered by vegetation that counteracts the heat island effect and provides additional insulation and cooling during the summer.

vermicomposting. The process where worms feed on slowly decomposing materials, like vegetable scraps, in a controlled environment to produce nutrient-rich soil.

VOC (volatile organic compounds). Carcinogens found in fabrics, paint, finishes, and synthetic foams. Most labels should indicate if a product has low or zero VOCs.

W–Z

watt (W). The standard unit of power for the International System of Units (SI). The watt determines the rate at which electrical energy is expelled.

WEEE (waste electrical and electronic equipment). Broken or unwanted electronic gadgets such as mobile phones or computers.

whole-house fan. A large fan that draws hot air up through the roof of a building and replaces it with cooler exterior air drawn from openings on lower floors.

wild harvested. Essential oils from herbs that are cultivated without chemicals or pesticides.

wind energy. Energy available from the pressure and currents of wind.

wind turbine. A wind energy conversion device with spinning blades that produce electricity.

windbreak. One or more rows of trees or shrubs that provide shelter from the wind and prevent soil erosion.

xeriscaping. Choosing plants and landscape greenery that do not require additional irrigation.

Index

A

air leaks 36–37, 78–79, 82–84, 100–01
alternative energy 40–43
alternative fuel. See fuel.
America 32–35
American
  energy use 33–34
    versus world 34
apartment 100–01, 196–201
appliances 47–49, 52–63, 101, 109
  Energy Star 13, 22, 50–51, 70, 110–11, 170
  kitchen 47–48, 52–59, 101
  laundry 60–63
audit, energy 36
  DIY 36
  air leaks 36–37
  blower door test 38
  cooling 38
  heating 38
  lighting 38
  professionals 38

B

babies 96–97
baking 142–43
  equipment 143
  organic 142
  sugar substitutes 142
bamboo 14, 17, 24, 28–29, 91
bathroom 23–24, 30–31, 100, 110–11
bedroom 30–31
  bedding 30–31, 93, 111

beer 147
  microbreweries 147
boiler systems 71
BTU (British thermal unit) 32–33

C

candles 31, 95
cars 149–165, 180–81
  air conditioning 152
carpooling 151
conventional 150–52
  electric 157
  flex-fuel 153
  hybrid 149, 154–55
  mileage 150–51, 154–55
  rentals 153
  tires 150
carbon
  emissions 16–17
  footprint 20–21, 27–28, 40, 76, 93, 102, 153
  offsets 92–93, 102–103
  reducing 22, 26–27
Casa Futura 85
Christmas 94–95
cities, green 200
  rural 173
cleaning 106–115
  appliances 109
  maintenance 110–11
  organic 108–09
clothing lines 17, 63
coal 40
coffee 146
  fair trade 46, 47, 91, 175, 84
  filters 146

mugs 146
organic 146
compact fluorescent lighting (CFL) see CFL
compost 17, 122–23
  apartment 101
worms 123
conservation 9, 12–13, 114–15
cork 14, 24, 29, 30

D

decorating 19, 22–25, 28–31
Department of Energy, U.S. 126
dining out 144–45
  carry out 145
  comment cards 145
  leftovers 145
  ocal 144
dishwashers 10, 23, 46–47, 49, 58–59, 110–11
drugs, prescription 185
dryers, clothing 49, 62
  dryer balls 62

E

emissions, carbon 16–17
energy consumption 46–65
energy efficiency 12–13, 46–48, 53, 64–65, 164
EnergyGuide label 50–51
Energy Star 13, 22, 50–51, 70, 100–01, 110–11, 170
EPA 40, 50, 170
event planning, green 88–89

Trademark Notices

This serves as an addendum to the trademark notice on page 2.

Avonite Surfaces ™ is a trademark of Aristech Acrylics, LLC.

Earth's Beauty™ is a trademark of Cosmetics without Synthetics.

EcoTop™ is a trademark of Klip Bio Technologies.

EnergyGuide© is a copyright of Nexus Energy Software.

EnergyStar™ is a trademark of the United States government (EPA and DoE).

EnviroGLAS® is a registered trademark of EnvironGlas Products, Inc.

The Glidehouse™ is a trademark of Michelle Kaufmann Design

JCPenney™ is a trademark of JCP Media L.P.

Marmoleum™ is a trademark of Forbo Holding

MaryJanesFarm® is a registered trademark of MaryJaneFarms, Inc.

Monopoly® is a registered trademark of Hasbro, Inc.

Nature's Grilling Products™ is a division of NRG International, LLC.

Organic Travel™ is a trademark of Organic Travel, Inc.

PaperStone™ is a trademark of Paneltech International, LLC.

Plyboo Neopolitan™ is a trademark of Smith & Fong Company

Richlite™ is a trademark of the Richlite Company.

EcoRowe™ is a trademark of Rowe Fine Furniture, Inc.

Simmons Mattresses™ is a trademark of the Simmons Bedding Company.

Squak Mountain Stone™ is a trademark of Tiger Mountain Innovations, Inc.

Thermos® is a registered trademark of Thermos LLC.

Vetrazzo® is a registered trademark of Vetrazzo, LLC.

Wicked Good Charcoal® is a registered trademark of Laralee Distributors, LLC.

ZipCar® is a registered trademark of ZipCar, Inc.

Acknowledgments and Photography Credits

The publisher would like to thank the following contributors, whose aid in creating this book was invaluable: Nancy Hajeski, Jennifer Acker, Phil Schmidt, David Goucher, Leslie Mertz, Beth Hanson, Kristin Maffei, Alice Hill, and Vrinda Manglik.

PHOTOGRAPHY CREDITS

The following abbreviations are used:
BSP—BigStockPhoto.com; JI—Jupiter Images; IO—IndexOpen.com; iSP— iStockphoto.com SS—Shutterstock.com; Wiki—Wikimedia Commons

T = top; b = bottom; c = center; l = left; r = right

Front Cover

background: iSP; roof: SS/Markus Gaan; house: top right iSP/Diane Diederich center right courtesy of Maytag; bottom right courtesy of Toyota; bottom center iSP/Darren Baker; bottom left courtesy of Motif Designs; center left iSP/Kameleon 2007; top left Stan Sudol; top center iSP/ Ken Hurst; center Jessie Walker

Back Cover

top right: SS/toriru; bottom left: JI; bottom right: SS/Joy Brown

Frontispiece

iSP/Darren Baker
Foreword
SS/ Manfred Steinbach

Chapter 1 THE GREEN HOME

8 JPS 10 JI 11 BSP/Michael Levy 12–15 John Swain Photography 16 SS/pxlar8 17l JI 17r JI

Chapter 2 TAKING STOCK

18 SS/Amra Pasic 20–21 Lisa Purcell 21b IO/DesignPics 22bl iSP/Kameleon 2007 22tr Wiki 23l Wiki 23tr SS/Baloncici 23br SS/Monika23 24br SS/Jorge Salcedo 24tl SS/Titi Matei 25bl JI 25br SS/Jay Lazarin 26tl JI

26bl SS/Rob Marmion 26r SS/Darren K. Fisher 27l SS/Kostantin Sutyagin 27r SS/lebanmax 28bl SS/Michael Letson 28t(a, b, c) fabricandart.com 28c Rowe Furniture 29tl www.co.contra-costa.ca.us 29tc www.co.contra-costa.ca.us 29tb www.co.contra-costa.ca.us 29tr Smith & Fong Plyboo 29br SS/Michael Pettigrew 30tl Vetrazzo 30bl (a, b, c, d) www.co.contra-costa.ca.us 30r Kushtush Organics 31tr SS/Aaron Stein 31br Beth's Boutique Candles 32 SS/Jaime Wilson 33 BP, "Statistical Review of World Energy," 2007 34 U.S. Department of Energy 35l SS/Travis Manley 35r IO/ Photos.com Select 36bl JI 36tr Wiki 38 Sage Homebuilders, St. Louis, MO 39 Flemming Lund/Infrared Diagnostic & Energy Audit 41 National Renewable Energy Laboratory 42 Courtesy of Verdant Power, copyright © 2007 43 National Renewable Energy Laboratory

Chapter 3 HUMMING ALONG

44 SS/Rob Marmion 46 Jonathan Conklin Photography 47 IO/Photos.com Select 48 JI 50 EnergyStar.gov 51 EnergyStar.gov 52 JI 53l SS/Anita 53r JI 54 SS/prism_68 55l JI 55r JI 56 JI 57t JI 57b Wiki/MECU 58 SS/g.lancia 59 SS/Irina Fischer 60 JI 61tl Wiki 61r JI 62bl SS/Chiyacat 62tr SS/Lara Barrett 63 SS/Peter Elvidge 64bl SS/Kameel4u 64tr SS/Anthony Berenyl 65t JI 65b Wiki 66 JI 67 SS/Polina Lobanova 68bl JI 68tr SS/Valentin Mosichev 69 SS/Robert J. Beyers II 70 SS/Xphantom 71 Wiki/W.L Tarbert 72bl SS/Keith McIntyre 72br SS/Colour 73 National Renewable Energy Laboratory 74 SS/Georgios Alexandris 75 Rinnai Corporation 76 WholeHouseFan.com 77l IO 77r Coolerado Corporation 78 JI 79 EnergyStar.gov 80 BSP/ Sherri Camp 81tl Wiki 81cl Wiki 81bl Wiki 81tr Wiki 81cr Wiki 81br JI 82 JI 83bl SS/SueC 83tr NFRC 85–86 ONteriors

Chapter 4 THE GREEN LIFESTYLE

86 SS/Stephen Finn 88t SS/ Gordon Swanson 88b JI 89bl Wiki/Romary 89tr JI 90tl JI 90br JI 91tl JI 91br JI 92c JI 92b SS/Hannamariah 93 JI 94 SS/Jason Stitt 95tl IO/Vstock 95br SS/Holly Kuchera 96tl SS/Heather